Prayers for Healing and Protection
A Gift from God

SHAKUNTALA MODI, M.D.

Strategic Book Publishing and Rights Co.

Strategic Book Publishing and Rights Co.
12620 FM 1960, Suite A4-507
Houston, TX 77065
www.sbpra.com

ISBN: 978-1-61897-947-6

Interior Book Design: Judy Maenle

When we pray, our prayers ascend through our connecting silver cord to God. God hears and answers our prayers through this "cosmic umbilical cord." Information is always flowing through this cord, whether we are aware of it or not. While individual prayers are important, group prayers have incredible impact. It is very important for family members to pray, both individually and together, for protection, healing, and guidance for themselves and all the people in their lives. Praying for other people sometimes is more powerful because it is selfless. All prayers are heard, no matter how superficial they are. Sometimes they are not answered right away or the way we want because there is a lesson to be learned from what is going on in our lives. God is all-knowing, but He will not interfere with our free will unless we ask. Asking for God's help is an exercise of our free will. Prayers are our open line to God. He will protect, heal, and guide us and will listen to and answer our prayers, but we must ask.

Other Books by
Shakuntala Modi, M.D.

Remarkable Healings: A Psychiatrist Discovers Unsuspected Roots of Mental and Physical Illness

Memories of God and Creation: Remembering from the Subconscious Mind

I humbly dedicate this book to God,
all the heavenly helpers and the whole humanity.
May it enlighten all the human beings
and expand their consciousness.

Acknowledgments

First, I acknowledge all my patients, through whom I was privileged to receive this amazing information. Their willingness to share this awesome knowledge is greatly appreciated. I am also thankful to Barbara Hamric for the hours of typing and retyping. She is a God sent help for me.

Ultimately, I humbly acknowledge God, all the heavenly masters, archangels, angels, heavenly guides, my higher self, inner self, and all the other heavenly beings for their enthusiastic and consistent participation, assistance, education, guidance, protection, and the gift of this book. As always, I am eternally grateful for this amazing privilege and all the blessings.

Table of Contents

Introduction: A Must Read

The Beginning

Perhaps many of you have not read my first two books, *Remarkable Healings* and *Memories of God and Creation*. Some background will pave the way for this, my third book, *Prayers for Healing and Protection*. I am a board-certified psychiatrist and have been in practice for about thirty-five years. Having learned during my residency that no one therapy worked for all patients, I set about exploring and perfecting the skills to use a variety of therapeutic approaches, depending on the varying needs and responses of my patients. Among these approaches are individual and group psychotherapy, family therapy, marriage counseling, psychodrama, transactional analysis, hypnosis, and hypnotherapy. I wanted to use them with patients to suit their needs for healing.

Over the years I used hypnosis and hypnotherapy with good results. Hypnosis allows patients to uncover the underlying subconscious reasons for their emotional, mental, and physical problems. The unresolved problems are brought from the subconscious mind to the conscious mind, and by recalling, reliving, releasing, understanding, and resolving the unresolved traumas and issues, the patients can be free from their long-standing problems, often in a few sessions.

Over the years of my psychiatric practice, I always felt good about the quality of my work and the results I had with my patients. I was able to help them with a combination of different treatment modalities, to suit their needs. But still there were some patients for whom I could not do much, except use medication and supportive psychotherapy. So I continued to search for ways to help my patients.

As described in my first book, *Remarkable Healings*, over the past twenty-five years, many of my patients have recalled past-life traumas as a source of their physical, emotional, mental, spiritual, and/or relationship problems. After recalling, reliving, releasing, and resolving the traumas and issues from one or more past lives, patients were relieved of their symptoms.

Over the years, I found many symptoms in my patients came from one or more past lives. Common among the problems that stem from past lives are psychosomatic disorders, deep-seated personality disorders and immune system disorders, with presenting symptoms, such as depression, anxiety, fears, phobias, panic attacks, premenstrual symptoms, sexual disorders, eating disorders, obsessive compulsive disorders, headaches, fibromyositis, arthritis, skin disorders, asthma, allergies, etc. *Remarkable Healings* is filled with many such case histories.

Many of my patients under hypnosis have reported finding human spirits inside them. They called them the visitors, spirits who have remained earthbound after the death of their physical body and were unable to make the transition to heaven after death. I found that I could converse with these guest spirits through my patients. They claimed to have remained on the earth because of love, hate, anger, jealousy, revenge, unfinished business, obsessive attachment to a person, a place or an object, or because of various forms of addiction, such as addictions to drugs, alcohol, gambling, food, or sex. They claim to be able to enter living people when their energy fields or auras were weakened because of many reasons, such as physical illness, anesthesia, surgery, or unconsciousness, or emotional conditions, such as anger, fear, hate, depression, grief, or anxiety. The spirits also explained they could enter patients who were using drugs and alcohol, playing video games, playing loud and discordant music, or who were engaging in a variety of occult activities, which included playing with Ouija boards, using automatic writing, channeling, or conducting séances without proper protection, or while playing conjuring games such as Dungeons and Dragons or Demons.

This was a particularly alarming revelation to me since most of us do not even know we have an aura that can be penetrated in such a manner. We all fall prey to illnesses, accidents, and an array of negative human emotions. These uninvited guests—that is, the possessing earthbound spirits, whether positive or negative—use living beings like motels on their way to heaven. They come in with all their baggage of physical, mental, and emotional problems, which are promptly transferred over to their hosts. What I was soon able to validate was that when these "cosmic hitchhikers" are released and sent on their way to heaven during treatment, they take their baggage, including all their emotional, mental, physical, and spiritual problems with them, leaving my patients free of their parasitic symptoms.

Many times my patients describe having demons in them, causing their presenting symptoms. My first encounter with a demon was through a patient who presented with chronic fatigue, depression, and migraine headaches, which had plagued him since adolescence. During the course of therapy, the patient said he saw a "black blob" in his head, which claimed to be a demon, a disciple of Satan, who was there to torture him. I was stunned because I had never encountered a demon of any kind personally and had no exposure to demons except through the movie *The Exorcist*. My patient acted nothing like that character. He was soft-spoken and polite. Once again on virgin territory, I decided to have a talk with the so-called demon to find out more about it. The demon said it had entered the patient during his adolescence when he was using drugs and was there to cause him headaches, chronic depression, and fatigue. There was no great drama about this dialogue, with the exception that patient's voice became very angry and his face mirrored a combination of hate and arrogance.

Once again, over the years many patients have reported seeing demons inside them in different parts of their bodies. The demons claimed to be the single most common cause for most psychiatric problems, such as depression, anxiety, panic attacks, suicidal or homicidal thoughts, fears, phobias, hallucinations, paranoia, delusions, etc. They project all their negativity, such as anger, hate, paranoia, violent sadomasochistic behaviors, desire for power and position, onto the patients, who in turn act out those thoughts and behaviors.

Angels have often affirmed through my patients that these demons are as real as they—the angels—are, but they are of negative energy and most of our emotional, mental, physical, marital, social, and relationship problems are caused by the demons' negative influence. They have consistently emphasized that every human being, specifically the doctors, including psychiatrists and all health care professionals, should pray daily for protection and guidance, because they do not know what they might be dealing with in their patients.

On a positive note, however, my hypnotized patients have consistently stated that although these demon spirits have great powers, with the help of God and the angels, we can be more powerful than Satan and his demons, which are only as strong as we allow them to be. Contrary to what we might suspect, Satan and his dark forces operate within the limitations.

Some patients described their soul fragmenting during different traumas, creating different symptoms for them. After resolving the trauma and retrieving the missing soul parts and integrating them back with the patient, they were healed.

Under hypnosis, my patients consistently reported seeing their souls located in the chest area, along with the heart. They view the soul as an immortal energy essence, a piece of God within us. Through the soul, God empowers the body. When our bodies die, our soul continues to live on, retaining all the memories. Patients have revealed that our soul fragments under stress, leaving holes in the soul that weaken the body and its aura. When that happens, people are especially vulnerable to negative influences and sickness. Typically, husbands, wives, parents, children, other relatives and close friends, and Satan and his demons are the frequent recipients and holders of soul parts. Some patients say their abusers also possessed their soul parts.

At the same time, patients report that they have soul parts belonging to other people. Usually, therapy is a stalemate until the soul parts are returned and restored to their owners. One thing I have become certain over the years is that to heal the mind and body, we must first heal the soul by removing the possessing spirits and soul parts of other people, resolving the current and past lives traumas, and retrieving and integrating the missing soul parts. Only then can we heal.

Let me clarify that having human and demon spirits in one's body and aura does not mean that the person is "evil." Our human frailty makes us all targets for spirit possession. It is simply a part of the human condition. According to the demons, people with a higher life purpose and those who are doing God's work are more often targeted by Satan and his dark forces, because they do not want those people to succeed with their purpose.

Belief in past lives, reincarnation, and demon and earthbound spirits, for either the patient or the therapist, is not at all necessary for the therapy to work. The patients do, however, have to be willing to go through the journeys of their subconscious minds, under hypnosis, in order to release those experiences and resolve their problems.

Over the years I have realized that we psychiatrists and other mental health professionals have a limited understanding about the true reasons for mental, emotional, and physical illness. I have learned to keep my mind open, to ask questions, and to stay away from giving my own interpretations during a session. I understand that the patient's subconscious mind not only has the knowledge of the reasons for their problems, but it can also provide solutions and even healing. After receiving similar information from a cross-section of my hypnotized patients for many years, I felt compelled to write about this mind-bending knowledge. My first book, *Remarkable Healings*, was the result.

Moving Along

The discoveries did not stop there. My hypnotized patients also began to provide astonishing information, resulting in my second book, *Memories of God and Creation*. It is the product of the compilation of the knowledge given by many hypnotized people. It answers almost everything we always wanted to know about God and creation—that is, how it happened and why, and everything since then. It is the history of our soul. This second book is only about the normal aspect of creation. The abnormal aspect of it will be described in a future publication.

Remarkable Healings dealt with a variety of therapeutic techniques in some detail, including hypnosis and hypnotherapy. Recognizing that many who read this book may not have read my first book, I offer here a synopsis of what hypnosis is and what it is not. The general public has many misconceptions and fears about hypnosis based on what they understand from television, motion pictures, and stage hypnosis. For people to benefit from the treatment, we need to dispel the misconceptions about hypnosis, so they can enter into therapy free from fear and with the correct expectations.

Hypnosis: Understanding the Subconscious Mind

Hypnosis is a state of focused concentration where we selectively block out peripheral awareness. To understand hypnosis and how it works, we need to understand our conscious and subconscious mind. The conscious mind is the thinking, reasoning, and problem-solving part of our mind, also known as the left brain. It is the part of our mind that deals with day-to-day functioning. It is the normal state of our awareness. The subconscious mind functions at a deeper level than our conscious mind and is known as the right brain. It deals with memories, intuition, and knowledge.

Normally, our conscious mind, or left brain, is cluttered with our day-to-day thoughts and problems. It is busy and constantly aware of everything that is happening around. In this state, we cannot bypass the conscious mind and get in touch with our subconscious mind to give suggestions or retrieve information.

The goal of hypnosis is to set aside our constantly chattering conscious mind. One way to do this is to guide people to focus on their breathing and relax different parts of their bodies. When the conscious mind is calm and quiet and not preoccupied by unnecessary thoughts, it is easy to bypass it and get in touch with the subconscious mind. Here the conscious mind is not asleep or unconscious, but it acts as a passive observer. It is aware of what is happening during a session, but it does not interfere with its doubts, constant analysis, and interpretations.

We achieve a similar state of focused concentration daily, normally and naturally, when we are absorbed in reading a book, watching a movie, listening to music, or driving on a highway (highway hypnosis) and lose track of time. Similarly, while day-dreaming, we are focusing on a person, place, or an event and are not concerned about our surroundings, nor are we distracted by the events near us. In these cases, our concentration is focused on whatever we are doing, and we are not asleep or unconscious.

Other times when we are in a state of deep hypnosis, including the moments just before we fall asleep and at the beginning stage of waking up in the morning.

Similarly when we are focusing on our emotional, mental, and physical problems, we are in a state of hypnosis. Most of the time when patients come to my office, they are suffering with intense emotions, such as anger, fear, sadness, or physical sensations, such as pain, numbness, palpitations, or difficulty breathing, or they use certain words over and over to describe their problems. In these cases, I usually ask them to focus on their emotional, mental, or physical feelings or thoughts and let those feelings and thoughts take them back to another time, to the source of the problems when they felt the same way. This can instantly bridge a present-time conflict to a conflict in the past, either in the current life or in a past life. Recalling, reliving, and resolving the trauma often free them of their problems. This is called the "bridge technique."

Thus, we can understand that during hypnosis people are not asleep or unconscious. They are in a state of focused concentration in which they are not aware of or paying attention to what is happening around them. Hypnosis itself is not a therapy. It is only a tool that can be used in therapy. Every hypnosis is self-hypnosis, just like the different examples of daily hypnosis described. We go in and out of the state of hypnosis several times every day without any formal induction. In therapy, a therapist only acts as a guide in assisting the patient, who controls the level of the trance and what is being revealed. The patients cannot act against their ethical or moral codes, and they can come out from under hypnosis any time they desire.

Hypnosis can be either directive or non-directive. In directive hypnosis, the therapist gives positive suggestions to help the patient, but the patient can accept or reject any of the suggestions, even at the deepest level of trance. One of the things I do for my patients is to make them a relaxation tape custom designed for their particular set of problems. In those tapes, I conduct a guided relaxation that takes patients into deep trance. Once there, I make a series of suggestions to address their particular needs in a positive way. While it works well and gives them relief, it is merely a symptomatic treatment. What a tranquilizer, a sleeping pill, or a pain pill can do, a relaxation tape with positive suggestions can also achieve in a motivated person, but they do not last for more than few days to few weeks.

Non-directive therapy, on the other hand, is where the life-altering changes can be made. I usually ask my patients to focus on their symptoms and let them take them back to a time when the problem or symptoms began. By getting in touch with their subconscious minds, patients can find the reasons for their problems, relive the events, resolve the emotions and physical traumas of those events, and ultimately release them. Therein lies the healing. It is easy for us to see how hypnotherapy is preferable to long-term traditional talk therapy and medication. It is quicker and has no side effects. Through the years, my patients have tapped into myriad of memories. They have brought many pieces of knowledge that are therapeutic, exciting, new, and are consistently reinforced, patient by patient. They have affirmed that the subconscious mind and the soul are one and the same and have all the memories of everything that has ever happened to us. Everything we have ever felt, sensed, heard, smelled, and experienced from the beginning of time is recorded in our soul, the subconscious mind. Nothing is erased, and we have the power and capability to recall any of these memories anytime we want to and need to.

With this understanding, we can realize why traditional talk therapy only works as a Band-Aid approach and is slow and less effective. During talk therapy, we deal with our conscious mind and knowledge, which is often superficial and based on intellectual interpretations. It is the subconscious mind that holds the understanding and knowledge about the real reasons for our current problems. Thus, we can see that the power to heal lies largely with that untapped portion of the human mind, the subconscious mind, or the soul. The subconscious mind is also the storehouse of our inner wisdom and knowledge that we all can tap into. It is our inheritance.

Mechanism of Receiving Information during a Hypnotherapy Session

Over the years, I have realized that patients' experiences during hypnotherapy vary widely. For some it is a firsthand, in-the-body experience, while for others there remains a degree of detachment, almost as if they were viewing a rerun on TV. Following are the different types of past-life experiences my patients have reported:

1. Sometimes patients see and hear nothing. The knowledge simply flows into them that they are now a different person, in a different place, and the meaning of the words that are spoken comes to them. They are aware of the feelings and the situations, but they really see or hear nothing. This is the most elemental way of perceiving.

2. Some patients report experiencing their past life as watching a movie, where they observe a life on the screen. In this case, they do not hear a voice but simply observe the action and receive the feelings and the knowledge from within, as in the first category.

3. In some cases, patients see the scenes being played out on a movie screen. They hear the voices, conduct the action, and receive the feelings and the knowledge from within.

4. In most advanced cases, patients report they actually entered the life and it is as if they are actually reliving it with the real people around them. They describe receiving the feelings directly, not just having the knowledge of the feelings. However, they also receive knowledge of the situation in the most elemental way, as in the first category. They have the perception of what is going on with other people rather than just the interpretation they have of that life. They have more knowledge in reliving and looking back than when they lived that life the first time.

9

The most important part in all the above examples is the fact that the patients receive the feelings and the emotional turmoil while perceiving the conflict going on. All of these experiences are therapeutic and promise success in releasing symptoms. As patients move up the scale in experiencing, the success of therapy increases.

During a past-life regression, patients often have parallel awareness of both the past life and the current life. At other times, they forget about the person they are now and go completely back into the former life, as in the most advanced case. Patients still can respond to my questions. They say that they are aware of me but have forgotten they have a self in the present.

Some patients relive every moment emotionally, physically, and mentally, screaming, crying, and sobbing in agony while reliving a traumatic movement. Others remain calm and unemotional while reliving the traumas. Either way, the experience can be therapeutic and can release the symptoms. However, it is much more effective when the patients relive and release the events emotionally, physically, and mentally by staying in that past-life body rather than watching from outside the body. Following are descriptions given by my patients.

- "In hypnotherapy sessions, I see in three different ways:

    1. I see some with the mind's eye. I concentrate and images are provided to me by my subconscious mind. Usually color and details are present, but it comes with hard work.
    2. I see as though I'm viewing a movie and images are rolling by, as if I'm viewing scenes in a movie. I am emotionally attached to some of the movie characters and the movie. Color, clarity, and details are present, but I'm not totally immersed in the event. Work is a little easier here.
    3. Sometimes when I'm in the flow, I am there! I hear the words! They come to me as a knowing. I do not hear voices, but I know what is being said. Things are real. Color, clarity, and details are fully present. I feel the feelings! I hear the sounds! I interact and react! I am there, and I am experiencing the event! Work is the easiest here."

- "Most of the time I see in my mind's eye and outside like a movie. I see people in their physical body, wherever it is, and then I see inside the body. I usually do not see the etheric field, but occasionally I do. I also do not see the aura normally except when the person is extremely sick. When I try to focus on what is happening all over the Earth or creation, I see in my mind's eye. I see a 3-D picture, like a holograph. Then when you ask me to look at somebody or something, I instantly see it like a movie. When you ask me to look at the creation, heaven, or a planet, first I see it in front of me because it is so big. Then when you ask me to look at a person, I see that person as in a 3-D movie and then I can see in that person's body. I do not even think I am instantly shown whatever I need to see. I feel that Archangel Raphael and my heavenly guides help with the visions and information."

Healing

- "Archangel Raphael is saying that there are three levels of healing, experiencing, and resolving the past life, seeing the spiritual content of the life, and its effects. There are past-life incidents that carry over, such as unresolved past-life emotions and decisions. At the same time, we have the individual and the group purposes that may or may not have been carried through. More often, it has not been carried through and will affect future lives. These are three different levels of healing that occur during a past-life regression therapy. They can all come from a past life: the physical incidents, emotional trauma, spiritual healing, or a lack of spiritual healing."

Role of Heavenly Helpers during a Hypnotherapy Session

During a hypnotherapy session, people receive different information in various ways. Often people can regress to an event in the current life or a past life and remember what was going on. Others are able to tap into that knowledge from the Akashic records, a repository of knowledge in heaven where all the information about the whole creation is recorded from the beginning of time. All our books are also included in the Akashic library, which contains our personal history since the creation of our individual souls. We can tap into our past, present, and even future lives, and any other information we want. People can also tap into other person's lives to do remote healing for these people.

During a hypnotherapy session, patients often claim they are receiving information from different heavenly beings, such as patients' heavenly guides, angels, higher selves, oversouls, masters, archangels, and other heavenly beings whose help we need. Patients often state during a session that their, and my, angels, guides, higher selves and other heavenly beings are always present helping, protecting, guiding, and giving information we need to heal the person, if we ask. If we do not ask, they just stay in the background until we ask for help. Sometimes patients receive information needed for their healing, but they are not aware of anybody helping them until they look around, and sure enough they see their angels, heavenly guides, masters, or other heavenly beings that are helping them.

Sometimes while working with earthbound human spirits and the demons, I also receive information in a backward way. I can communicate with these possessing spirits through the patients and get information from them. Demons after their transformation are willing to co-operate and give different information about the dark side, Satan and his plan, and why they want to stop me from writing these books. According to the demons, so far they are very successful in making humans believe that Satan and his demons are not real and are only figments of humans' imagination. The demons are afraid that through these books, I will tell people about the reality of Satan and his demons, that they are real, how they affect us, and how we can free ourselves from them.

According to archangels, ultimately we are getting information directly from God through masters, oversouls, our guides, angels, higher self, and other heavenly beings funneled through the archangels and sent through the patients telepathically.

While working with human and demon spirits, patients often are aware of multitudes of angels, archangels, masters, and other heavenly beings present in and around the room, depending on what we are working with. Sometime if we are working with a very large demon who may be a big commander in Satan's hierarchy and has trained and commanded multitudes of demons on Earth and in other dimensions, then after the transformation into the Light, it is more than happy to call out all those demons it commanded and trained. Patients describe seeing millions and trillions of demons coming from all over the Earth and other planets, transforming into the Light and going to the Light (heaven). During this time, patients often see the whole heaven opening up with archangels, Michael, Gabriel, Raphael, and Uriel, at the entrance of heaven, and other angels miles and miles around. Sometimes they see God as a pyramid or a mountain of Light and masters of our planet in front of him. Patients describe that they were watching and helping us because this was supposed to be a long-awaited historical event.

Working with these therapies for about twenty-five years, I have learned that every individual has at least one to three or more guardian angels and heavenly guides assigned, depending on our purpose. They are always with us to guide and protect us as soon as our soul enters the Earth environment and the womb. But they cannot do anything until we ask for help. According to heavenly beings, God gives every individual a free will, and God and other heavenly beings cannot interfere with our free will and cannot help us unless we ask. Heavenly beings often insist that I should tell everybody I work with, and write in the books, of the importance of prayers. "We are just a thought away from you," they say, "and can be instantly with you and help you, but if you do not ask for help we just watch you suffering and cannot interfere with your free will. Even if somebody prays for help for another person, the help will be provided to that person. So pray for help regularly for yourself and your fellow human beings, and even for beings of other dimensions, and the help will be given." Heavenly beings, over the years, have given "protection prayers" that are included in my two books, *Remarkable Healing* and *Memories of God and Creation*.

I learned to pray regularly every day and also before and during the sessions. I invoke the power and presence of God, all the masters, archangels, other angels, and heavenly beings whose help we need to protect and help us. I have this deep inner faith that they are always there when we ask for them, and patients often confirm their presence. I do not see or hear beyond the five physical senses, but I have an inner knowing about different things, and I am often aware that my heavenly guidance comes through what seems to be my own thoughts. Any information I need to heal patients and what I need to know for the books is given internally from my inner self or from the outside from heavenly helpers.

Many times when we get stuck in a session, I pray for guidance, or for a technique to get through patient's blocks, and sure enough, new ideas and techniques come to my mind. With God, anything is possible. Any information and understanding we want is given to us. We are given an understanding about various issues as well as a lot of higher spiritual knowledge. Wisdom that was previously given to few selected prophets is now given to anybody who desires it and is ready to receive it.

Sometimes during the sessions with certain patients there are four archangels, Michael, Gabriel, Raphael, and Uriel, who are always present to protect, heal, guide, and give us the knowledge we need. One of my patients described them as follows:

- "There are four archangels who are often present during a session. They are Michael, Gabriel, Raphael, and Uriel. They appear in a guise that is acceptable to the person they reveal themselves to. They can appear differently to different people. Archangel Michael appears to me as being about thirty years old, six feet three inches tall, of medium build, with blue eyes and blond hair, cut in a normal man's cut. His face is triangular. His skin is white. He looks like a Scandinavian. He projects an air of quiet efficiency and a stern, steely determination. Most of the time he seems to be serious and completely task oriented. It is his job to oversee the protection of the universe from dark and evil forces. He is also in charge of the angels and archangels.

"Archangel Gabriel appears as a thirty-five year old man about six feet two inches tall with a sturdy build, with black curly hair cut short and with dark brown eyes. He has a rectangular face. His skin color appears to be like that of a Persian or East Indian. He is also quietly efficient but not as serious as Michael. He is often smiling and projects an air of loving acceptance. His specialty, as far as we are concerned, is a combination of the spiritual and religious aspects of humanity.

"Archangel Raphael appears as a man who might be thirty-one or thirty-two with brown hair in a full cut, light brown eyes, a rectangular face, and olive complexion. He is about six feet one inch tall with a strong build. Raphael looks like a Spaniard or an Italian or perhaps a Greek. He looks as if he might play tackle on a small college football team. He is frequently smiling and laughing. There is an air of warmth and love about him. He seems to be very accepting of humanity and the human condition. His specialty is humanity in the universe and human affairs.

"Archangel Uriel appears older than the other archangels, seeming to be a man of about fifty-five. He has some gray hair at the temples and mostly with brown hair and brown eyes. He seems to be about 6 feet tall and with a medium build. His oval face has some lines in the white skin. He looks like a Slavic or a Siberian. He does smile some. He looks at everything at one time and ties it all together. He specializes primarily in alien races and the interconnections with the humankind. He also specializes in the physical world in technology and science."

During a session, some patients state that in addition to the four archangels, sometimes there is a whole host of heavenly beings who are present on the sides. Some of them are masters, oversouls, and other heavenly beings that specialize in the information we are working on during that session. They have often chosen to be there to give us the information we need. They are the ones who decide what information the patient needs for healing, what I need to heal my patients, and also what I need for the books. Sometimes patients say that during a session there are many human observers present in heaven. These humans are often currently incarnated on Earth and their souls have come to heaven to observe and learn from what we are doing during the session. One of my patients under hypnosis gave the following information about these cosmic helpers and observers:

- "I am in heaven with the archangels Michael, Raphael, Gabriel, and Uriel. I see there is a helpers' gallery on the left; these are different masters, oversouls, angels, guides, and some human souls who have an interest in what we are doing and have information to contribute. These beings on the panel are the source of information and help us directly through the archangels. There are about forty-one different beings helping us today. Information is given by them to the archangels telepathically, and then the archangels channel it through me either as a thought, a picture, a feeling, a symbol, or whatever is the best way to communicate. Quite often I see a picture, and then the information is supplied surrounding the picture. When I connect with the picture, it is like entering into it and knowing what is going on there. It is as if I am a participant."

Sometimes during a session, the four archangels are present constantly for hours at a time to help us. I wondered why four of the important busy archangels are always present for hours with us during the session. They must have much more important work to do. So I asked them about it. Archangel Michael explained it as follows:

- "It is possible for us to be moving so quickly that we appear to be present constantly in one place. We are in many different places at the same time. This is a property of angels and, in fact, also a property of demons, but they do not remember it, because they rejected God and do not use it. We are here and also at the other places at the same time. We are fully present here but only for a fraction of an instant then we leave and go somewhere else. We make fifteen to twenty stops, attend to different things, and are fully present in that place and back here in an instant. There is no observable time when we are not here. Our capabilities are beyond your comprehension. To you we appear to be constantly here, but we can be in many places at the same time.

"We are all assigned by God to be here to help you, because this is some of the most important work at this time, and we are instructed to help you. It is not the first time God's truth is given, and it will not be the last. In each case, the truth is tailored to a particular type of population, for those who are ready to perceive it. It is important to God that this information is brought out to the world. You are one of the chosen vessels, and you are doing quite well. God is very pleased, and we all are very pleased also. It is our pleasure and privilege to be here to work with you.

"We specialize in different things, and we want you to have a fully rounded picture of everything. Uriel is giving the information about aliens and about the physical and biological sciences, putting them into action. Raphael is helping with the things that deal particularly with humanity. Gabriel special- izes with spirituality and religion and helping you with those aspects, and I am providing integration and an overview of all the aspects that are involved in this.

"The information is coming from more than one source, to more than one person. Sometimes the explanations can be different. If two sources of information, which are extremely similar, follow exactly the same pattern, then it is beneficial to read them both, because they will present different aspects of the same thing. They will show things in a way that is perhaps in keeping with different types of people, a different under- standing of the same. It is advisable that people read from more than one source.

"All of these heavenly beings are asked to be here by God to give you different types of knowledge. Most of them will be here regardless, because of how they feel about your work and its importance to our objectives. Many of them are masters, oversouls and other beings. They are knowledgeable in the areas you are dealing with and have chosen to do this work of giving the information to you. Some of the oversouls and masters are connected to you and the patients you are working with, but most of them are here because they have information to share. They are sending the information that you need to know, through us archangels then through the patient to you.

"You are receiving the information from heaven and incorporating it in your books. The basic structure and the framework of the books you have already prepared in heaven, before incarnating into the current life, and it is being given back to you. It is like reminding you of different things that you already knew before coming into incarnation but have forgotten. These beings are also providing you some new information, which you need to integrate in your books."

Shift of the Planet Earth and Humanity to the Fifth Dimension

While doing this work for about twenty-five years, some of my patients were able to tap into the future events from the Akashic library in heaven. Some people saw events before and during December 2012 and the shift of planet Earth and humanity from the third dimension where we are now to the fifth dimension. During a session, I asked Archangel Michael who was helping us.

DR. MODI: Michael, can you tell us about what will happen in December 2012?

ARCHANGEL MICHAEL: In December 2012, there will be a shift. Earth, sun, and the center of the galaxy are aligning with each other. A new higher dimension has been opened up for Earth that was not available before. People will have access to it. It is already there, but nobody is there yet.

When you humans make the transition to the higher dimension, you will have no dark influences, will not be influenced by sickness or aging, and you will not die because of aging or some outside force, but you will choose to leave. You will communicate regularly with the Light and with one another through telepathy. Some will choose not to go into the fifth dimension because they do not believe in God or are afraid to go because they are influenced by demons.

Each person has to make a conscious choice to move or not to move into the fifth dimension. The Earth will also have a chance to make a choice to make a shift. Everybody will need help. That is why everybody will have to work together at this time. The new fifth dimension will have different vibrations. The environment will be more pleasing and healthy. The Earth movement will not happen on its own. It will need help, and groups of people will need to work with Earth to move it into the fifth dimension.

Satan and his demons will also make a last-minute effort to hold people back by causing fear and chaos. They will create darkness. People will panic, and they will try to go back to the dimension they were in. People can choose to come back at any time, but they will not want to come back once they are there.

One month before 12-12-12, seven seals (seven chakras) will open, and the information will be given to everybody. Then what they do with that information is up to them. They will be told who they are, and in the next dimension, we will be functioning at a higher level. People will be given the knowledge of themselves in relation to the entire universe. It will be on a much broader scale. God will also help them to understand not to be afraid that they have a closer relationship to the universe and to the Light. They will be given a time when it will happen and when they will have to make a conscious decision whether they want to move or not.

Each person will spend more time with one chakra or other. God will be speaking to each person individually, in the way most convenient to them based on where they are in their chakras or spiritual growth. The way information will be given to each person will be different for different people, the way they can comprehend, and in a language they can understand.

Seven seals will be opened by seven angels, for everybody to fully get the information. People will still doubt the information they will receive, because they will get all the information in less than a second, and it will be easy for them to doubt. That is why your job will be very important. You need to make people aware of what will happen on 12-12-12, but also of what will happen a month before. They need to be aware of it and acknowledge it; otherwise, it will be very easy for people to dismiss it as a dream. Unless people consciously pull out the information they receive through the opening of the seven seals, they will be open to doubts.

Darkness will occur because of the planetary shift, but Satan and his demons will manipulate what will happen during that darkness by creating panic and fear during that time.

DR. MODI: What will happen on planet Earth?

ARCHANGEL MICHAEL: There is a possibility of a large famine all across the planet and many people will die of hunger. There will be infectious diseases around 2012, causing a lot of death. There will be lots of floods and fires because of the heat and lots of dry land because of the lack of moisture. This is already starting in the West. It will be much more widespread. Flooding will happen on all the coastlines of the world, and many people will drown. Lots of land will be submerged in the ocean because of the rise in the level of water over the Earth. Asteroids hitting the planet and nuclear attacks can be prevented.

Many people will die and those who survive will get a chance to make a decision. Those who are in heaven will also get a chance to make a decision.

Remember through prayers, most of the death and destruction can be prevented. So tell people to pray for help and healing. If people are not ready and do not chose consciously, the actual shift may not happen at this time. What you can do is lessen people's suffering by educating them that death is not the end. Many of these catastrophes will happen because of the changes in the planet, but most of them will happen because of the demonic influences. Satan is aware of what is going to happen on 12-12, and all the demons will take advantage and cause as many problems as possible before the shift occurs.

Satan's plan is to distract people. He wants all these catastrophes to occur, so that everyone will be running around trying to cope with the disasters, and 12-12-will arrive and there will be nobody there to move into another dimension. It is very important to find the best strategy to inform as many people as you can before the shift to another dimension occurs.

You need to let people know that God and Light are much more powerful than Satan and his demons can ever be. God and the whole heaven are already helping tremendously, so the earth and all humans can shift from the third dimension, where you are now, to the fifth dimension successfully. Heaven has never been as busy from the beginning of creation as it is now to help planet earth and humanity with the shift.

New Commandments or Golden Principles

During one session, Archangel Michael said that I need to put "Golden Principles" in the introduction chapter of my third book because when we move into the fifth dimension, the old Ten Commandments will not apply anymore. He gave the following information:

ARCHANGEL MICHAEL: The commandments or rules of God are about to change. There will be a new revised edition when human beings move into the fifth dimension. That means that the old commandments, such as "thou shall not lie," will not apply anymore in the fifth dimension nobody will be able to lie, because everybody will be telepathic. One's words will always contain love and kindness. Anger, blame, and criticism will not be a part of the Golden Principles. Basically they [the Golden Principles] will vibrationally raise a person's consciousness. They will not demand an allegiance to God. Instead, they will be the pure spiritual principles of the Light. Every person will have to earn free will in order to evolve. It will not be granted automatically. By then human beings should be evolved enough to figure out its application for love, kindness, emancipation, and growth. It will happen when humans and the whole planet Earth shift into the fifth dimension.

In the fifth dimension, the Akashic records will be opened up, and Light will be available to everybody. People will be allowed to tap into information from it. People will have most of their memories. Death will not be feared. People will choose to leave their bodies after their purpose is finished.

The old commandments are more rigid, such as "Thou shall not covet thy neighbor's wife." That was for the mentality of the time. "Honor your father and mother" will be changed to "Honor yourself and the 'I am' in all others." The Golden Principles need to be written in the positive framework. There should not be a "not" word. For example, "Thou shall always speak truthfully and kindly" instead of "Thou shall not lie."

The Golden Principles must be put in writing right away. You need to put them in your third book, on the Internet, and place them everywhere. They will be the replacement for the old commandments. You should be talking to everyone, because these principles can be lived all the time and are not situational. They are an attitude and are like spiritual practices.

This patient was among the seven ladies in a cave-like setting who wrote the original Ten Commandments and gave them to Moses. The old commandments talked about specific situations such as "Thou shall not kill," and "Thou shall not steal." These are like commands and are negative. The new ones will be positive, to invite the soul into the Light. They speak only of kindness and are very simple to follow. They need to be shared with everybody and will shift everybody's consciousness. There are no rules and regulations and no punishment in the Golden Principles.

In fact, the original Ten Commandments were somewhat demonically influenced because of the negativity in the use of the words such as "Thou shall not kill." It created the energy that a person has to have the knowledge of killing in order to kill. So they will allow the demons to enlighten them about killing even if they did not know.

These new principles are not commandments, but are conscious choices. Their vibrations are higher. A commandment is an order or rule of an authority, as you say in transactional analysis, the parent telling the child what to do. When you put the old commandments and the new golden principles side by side, people can see the evolution. The new ones are s and positive, and even a child can follow them. You d have to know anything negative in order to practice them. This is what God desires. You need to send these around the world on the Internet. You will be given the credit for invoking these Golden Principles. It is about learning that we are all part of God, rather than God as a vindictive, punishing God, which was in reality invented by Satan.

The information is channeled through the intention of living that way yourself, Dr. Modi, and you are living it. It is all right to take credit for being part of God. That is not ego. That is Light. Humans, when they get filled with Light, feel powerful, not in the sense of ego but as an awesome awareness of God. When He shares His Light and knowledge with people, they feel empowered. You must put your palm out and say, "I humbly share this gift of knowledge with love, Light, and kindness." And you are filled with Light. You are humble in it. Your ego is not in it, only your heart.

Old Commandments

1. I am the Lord your God: you shall not have strange gods before me.
2. Thou shall not take the name of the Lord your God in vain.
3. Remember to keep holy the Lord's Day.
4. Honor your father and your mother.
5. Thou shall not kill.
6. Thou shall not commit adultery.
7. Thou shall not steal.
8. Thou shall not bear false witness against your neighbor.
9. Thou shall not covet your neighbor's wife.
10. Thou shall not covet your neighbor's goods.

Golden Principles

1. Pray for yourself and all others every day.
2. Find time to be still and meditate every day.

3. Honor yourself and the "I Am" in all others.
4. Bring the Light to wherever you go.
5. Have an altar in your home.
6. Give all giving from your heart.
7. Embrace every being in the entire creation of God for the new world.
8. Allow the world to be as it is, not as you want it to be.
9. Every thought must come from energy of love. So when you speak a thought, you feel the emotion of love first, and then the words are spoken with love.
10. Make peace with everybody at home and everywhere around you.

According to heavenly beings, I need to publish all this information for the general public. Then they can pray for the healing of themselves and everybody on planet Earth, so we can all heal ourselves and others with prayers, and make a successful transition from the third dimension to the fifth dimension. We cannot move into the fifth dimension with our baggage of anger, hate, jealousy, desire for revenge, and all the negative thoughts and behavior that have lower vibrations and will not be allowed into the higher dimensions. Come with me and explore these amazing techniques and prayers for healing and protection given through the love of God and watch the miracles happen.

None of the information presented in this book comes from my religious or cultural background or from any of my personally held beliefs. It is based solely on what hundreds of my patients have consistently reported under hypnosis. One of the most impressive results is the universality of the information obtained. Although most of the people reporting the information come from diverse cultural, religious, socioeconomic, and educational backgrounds, the information they received under hypnosis is strikingly similar and consistent. Even young children and teenagers have given similar information. Their words may differ, the expression may vary, but the basic information is the same, woven of common threads into the same essential themes.

The word "Light" is used synonymously for God, Heaven, and for the emanation of Light coming from Heaven. The letter "L" in the word "Light" is capitalized to differentiate it from the regular, earthly light, and also because patients describe God and Heaven as just pure white Light. Also, throughout this book, I have addressed God as "He" and "It" because that is what my patients called Him.

Development of Healing and Protection Prayers

Over the years, my hypnotized patients, who come from different cultures, religions, and educational backgrounds, consistently described that we begin our journey for spiritual development as a pure soul, a piece of God. We plan and live many lives to go through different experiences for our spiritual growth. During each life, with different emotional, mental, and physical traumas, our soul fragments, and we lose thousands of soul parts creating the holes in our soul. This causes a weakness in our soul and thus in our body. These holes create the openings in the body that are occupied by human, demon, and other spirits, causing physical, emotional, mental, and relationship problems. I realized that to heal the mind and body, we need to heal the soul, first by removing the human and demon spirits and the negative energies. Then to heal these holes in the soul, we need to resolve the current and past lives traumas, retrieve all the lost soul parts that we lost in different lifetimes, and heal and close the holes, thus preventing any further infestation by the outside spirits. By healing the soul, we can heal the mind and body.

As described in my first book, *Remarkable Healings*, earthbound and demon spirits claimed to come inside my patients when their aura—the electromagnetic energy field around them—was weakened due to different conditions. Physical conditions such as sickness, anesthesia, surgery or accidents, and emotions like sadness, fear, anger, hate, depression, anxiety, compassion, and grief can make a person's aura weak and vulnerable for spirits to enter. Use of drugs and alcohol is one of the biggest reasons for spirit attachment; sometimes just using them once can open the shield around us. The aura-electromagnetic shield can also weaken or have holes when people hear loud and disharmonious music or engage in a variety of occult activities, such as playing with Ouija board, doing automatic writing, channeling, or conducting séances without proper protection, as described in detail in *Remarkable Healings*. Please read it for a better understanding.

Following drawings are taken from my first book, *Remarkable Healings*. Please examine them carefully to understand how the problems and diseases are caused and what can we do to heal them.

HEALTHY AURA (ENERGY FIELD AROUND THE BODY) AND THE SHIELD

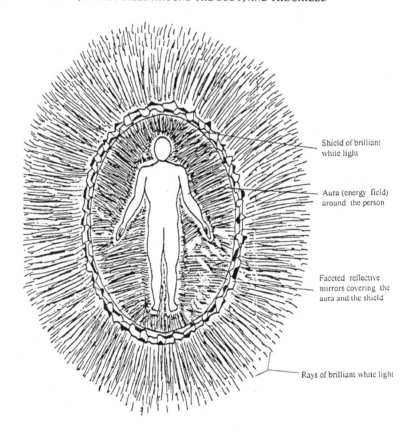

Shield of brilliant white light

Aura (energy field) around the person

Faceted reflective mirrors covering the aura and the shield

Rays of brilliant white light

Aura   The aura looks like a buffer zone around me (a person). It consists of a solid mass of white light about 18 - 20 inches thick. It consists of thin densely arranged rays that look almost like a shaft of wheat in consistency.

Shield   The shield appears as an oval shaped protective mirror that looks faceted. Light reflects off of the shield in many directions and for a long distance.

27

POSSESSION BY EARTHBOUND ENTITIES

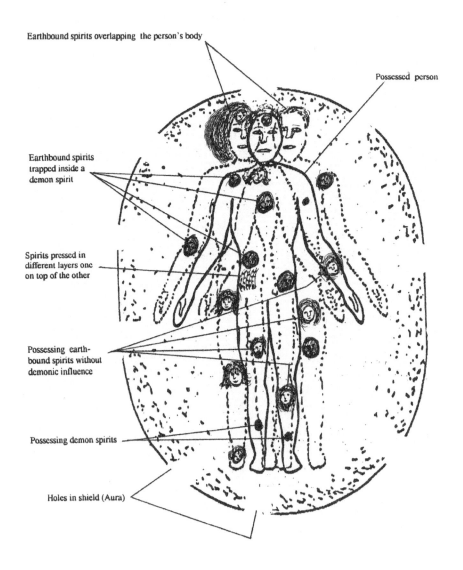

Earthbound spirits overlapping the person's body

Possessed person

Earthbound spirits trapped inside a demon spirit

Spirits pressed in different layers one on top of the other

Possessing earth-bound spirits without demonic influence

Possessing demon spirits

Holes in shield (Aura)

POSSESSION BY DEMON ENTITIES

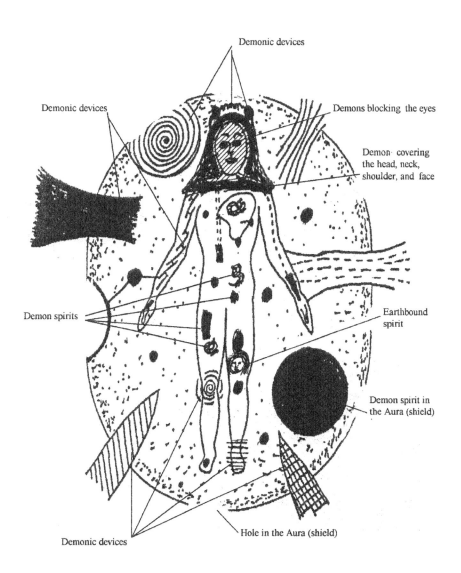

Demonic devices

Demonic devices

Demons blocking the eyes

Demon covering the head, neck, shoulder, and face

Demon spirits

Earthbound spirit

Demon spirit in the Aura (shield)

Demonic devices

Hole in the Aura (shield)

SOUL FRAGMENTATION AND SOUL LOSS

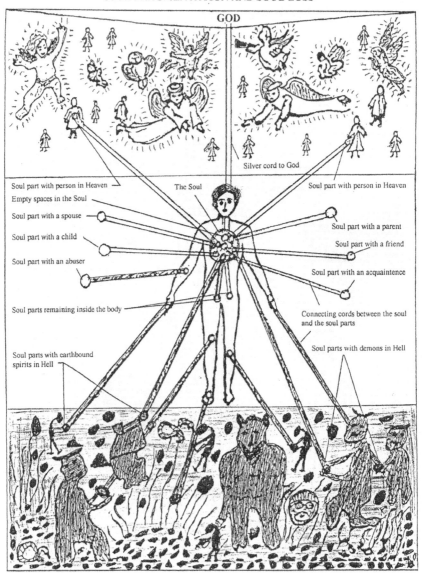

General Protection Prayers

As I began to recognize, locate, and release human and demon spirits from my patients, I realized that just by being human we are all open for spirit attachment, because we all get angry, sad, anxious, scared, depressed, become sick, have surgeries or accidents, or use drugs and alcohol. I began to wonder about how we could protect ourselves. My patients often reported seeing angels, masters, and other heavenly beings that helped us while we were releasing spirits. Wondering about Satan and his demons, which many of my patients reported seeing, I asked Archangel Gabriel, who was helping us, whether Satan and his demons are real or not, and if real, who they are.

ARCHANGEL GABRIEL: Yes they are as real in the invisible world as we are, but they are of very negative energy. They are the lost souls. You need to treat them as patients, and you need to help them to see the Light within them. These demons can cause different types of physical, mental, emotional, relationship, and other problems for humans. All psychiatrists and other physicians, therapists, and all the other health professionals should pray for protection and guidance regularly every day, because they do not know what they are dealing with.

DR. MODI: How we can protect ourselves from human and demon spirits and their influences

ARCHANGEL GABRIEL: Protection can be invoked in many ways. The first and most important and basic of the protection techniques is prayer. Pray to God to cleanse, heal, shield, protect, guide, and bless you. Turning the mind to God and the Light provides the first layer of defense and shielding against the demonic attacks. The mind that is turned to God and the Light will eliminate half of the possible demonic attacks. The next important form of protection is to form an intent not to be possessed and influenced by Satan and his demons and to reject all their works and everything that is evil and dark. Also, to accept the work of God and achieve His purposes by dedicating your life to Him.

31

Shakuntala Modi, M.D.

When you dedicate your life to God, it establishes a strong connection and constant communication back and forth between you and God. That means you will always be in the Light.

You should also pray for your family members, friends, coworkers, and other people you care for, and even for people with whom you have problems. When everybody around you is free of negative influences and is protected, you can live in peace and harmony with each other. Also, remember to pray for protection for your surroundings, such as your home, workplace, and cars.

All human beings have their own guardian angels assigned to protect and guide them, but we angels cannot do anything unless you ask us for help. God gives everybody free will, and we cannot interfere with your free will. If you do not ask us for help, we cannot help, but when you ask, we are instantly there to help you. We are just a thought away from you and can be with you instantly.

Request your angels to remove all the earthbound, demon and other entities, dark shields, dark energies, dark devices, and dark connections from your body, aura, soul, and cord, and also from your home, workplace, places of recreation, cars, and everything in them and miles and miles around them. Then ask them to fill and shield you, your home, workplace, and cars with brilliant, white, crystalline Light. Request them to plug all the holes and tunnels in you and your surroundings and cars.

As the angels do that, you should visualize a column of dazzling, shimmering, vibrant, white, crystalline Light coming from above your head and filling your whole body, cleansing and healing every part, every organ, and every cell of your body. If you cannot visualize it, you can just imagine it, and it will be so.

Then imagine this white, crystalline Light spreading an arm's length all around you, below your feet, above your head, in front of you, behind you, and on both sides of you, creating a bubble of white, crystalline Light all around you. Then visualize this bubble covered by the reflective spiritual mirrors and rays of shimmering white Light all around. These demons

32

are afraid of the Light; they think they will be burned and killed by it. So if you visualize or imagine yourself like a brilliant, blinding hot afternoon sun several times a day, every day, you can keep them away from you. Similarly, visualize your home, workplace, cars and places of recreation being cleansed, filled and shielded by the brilliant, white, crystalline Light and imagine them looking like a blinding afternoon sun. Ask your angels to stay on guard around you and your surroundings as long as your soul exists. You should also pray for your family members, friends, co-workers, and even the people with whom you have problems and their surroundings.

All human beings have energy centers (chakras), which can also be infested and blocked by entities and negative energies. You should routinely ask your angels to cleanse, heal, balance, and open up all your energy centers when needed and cover and protect them when not needed.

Humans also have many spiritual channels of communication with God, masters, higher self, guides and angels, which can be infested with entities and negative energies and can be blocked and have holes. So request your angels regularly to cleanse, heal, shield, and protect all your channels of communication with the Light (heaven).

Also, stay away from drugs, alcohol, and intense emotions that can open your shield for those entities to come in.

Use these protection prayers at least twice a day, every night before sleeping and in the morning after you wake up, and you will be protected. Remember, we do not come until we are called, so call upon us and we shall be there instantly. We are just a thought away.

Dedicating Our Lives to God

According to the heavenly beings, during prayer we can form an intent to accept the work of God and achieve God's purposes by dedicating our lives to God. Many people are afraid that if they dedicate their lives to God, they will have to give up their possessions and loved ones and go to a remote place to pray and meditate, as some saints did in the past. This is not true. When we dedicate our lives to God and God's purposes, this establishes a strong connection and ensures constant communication back and forth between us and God. This means we will always be in the Light and will be guided by God and the heavenly beings in the right direction every day.

When we dedicate our lives to God, we are also giving our permission to Him and the heavenly beings to help and guide us in the right direction. God gives everybody free will. As a result, unless we ask God and heavenly beings for help, they cannot help us. By dedicating our lives to god, we exert our free will. However, this will not mean that all our actions will be correct and all our thoughts will be noble. Because of our human frailties and the dark influences, we will still be prone to make mistakes, but by asking for God's help, we can be protected and directed toward the right path. Here is a prayer to use to dedicate our lives to God:

"Dear God, I intend to dedicate my life to you from this day on. Please protect and guide me every day, so I can fulfill your will. Please keep me on the right path and help me in achieving the goals and purposes I planned for this life. Thank you."

My patients gave the following descriptions of what they saw under hypnosis when I prayed.

- "I saw the angels removing all the foreign spirits, dark devices, and energies from people with their nets of Light and then cleansing and filling them with the Light and bringing their soul parts back and integrating them. With the silver connecting cords, I saw angels with a device like a corkscrew, taking the blockage out like a cork out of a wine bottle. Then they healed the cords and put the cylinder of Light around them. I saw them cleansing and healing the whole Earth and all the dimensions throughout the creation, bringing their soul parts and integrating them with those to whom they belong."

- "When you asked to help all the earthbound human spirits up into the Light, some of those influenced by dark entities refused to go with the angels, but multitudes of earthbound spirits chose to go to the Light. Some of them had been lost for centuries, in dwelling places, in the spots where they died violently, in the hospitals, from around funeral homes, graveyards and the battlefields where they were killed, looking very dazed and confused and not knowing what had happened, and many were wandering around on the Earth.

Sometimes the lost human spirits were so self-focused and self-involved that they could not even look to the Light. When the soul parts were brought back to them, they started to look around. The higher the vibration of the universe, the less lost souls there are. As you go down in vibration in the universes, the number of the lost beings is higher."

- "When you asked everybody to be shielded, the shield formed around everyone. With some, it left immediately because they did not want it. They also protected planets and various bodies in space, such as asteroids, stars, etc. I saw tubes of Light forming around our universe and some of the other universes, around each galaxy, planetary system, and dimension, including Earth and everybody and everything in it. I saw angels scrubbing, brushing, and cleansing the surfaces."

- "When you asked for cleansing, healing, and blessing food and drinks, it was done. There is spiritual energy that goes into growing the food, and that energy comes from food to us as we consume it. These things happen naturally. As plants grow and fruit and grains are formed, it is filled with the spirit of God— the spiritual energy. As we eat them, that energy comes to us. I understand that genetic modification weakens the plants, especially when not done according to God's plan."

- "When Dr. Modi asked for all the dark entities, energies, and devices to be suctioned out, I saw a big vacuum cleaner suctioning out all the dark energies from throughout the creation. Then when she asked all the soul parts of people and other souls and places to be brought back from them, I saw all the soul parts in the dark energies being sucked out in the opposite direction, going back where they belong and integrated after complete cleansing and healing."

- "Today, when the soul parts were coming back, I felt so much emotion. I saw golden Light around the soul parts. They were large misty-looking groups of soul parts coming back, and they were going to groups of people, like family, people at work, medical profession, film business, spiritual and religious groups, etc."

Inter- and Intra-dimensional Pathways

An attack can be launched through the spiritual dimensions in which demons and angels travel freely. This has the effect of bypassing the shield around the person. In spite of the shield being intact, demons can enter a person's body through other dimensions. According to the angels, they do so from certain spots between those dimensions; they cannot do so from just anywhere. Demons can also shove devices from those dimensions to this dimension, and they appear in us. These other dimensions are like other universes with vibrations similar to our universe. In these cases, we should request the angels to shield those areas and stay on guard around those certain spots between the two dimensions. My patients gave the following descriptions.

- "I saw the inter-dimensional pathway that is like going from one rate of vibration to another rate of vibration, and in between is this layer of change of vibration that pervades everywhere. So the inter-dimensional pathway is not a portal or a door. It is all over the place, and it is not what we think of as a path. When you asked them to be protected just like each of the dimensions, they were flooded with the Light."

- "As Dr. Modi prayed for protection for inter- and intra-dimensional pathways, I saw dimensions vertical to our dimension where before I used to see them horizontal. The vertical dimensions are open at the top. At first, I saw energy pulling and pushing out, but it is actually a cord to the higher level. The connecting cord to God is very apparent in each alternate reality, so the aliens are no longer preoccupied with interfering with or even accessing our dimension. If people here need to access the alternate reality, they will have to go through with some efforts consciously. Inter- and intra-dimensional pathways are not really the pathways. They are bleeding through, because they are aligned on top of one another. Now they are all straight, so the connection has to be much more deliberate from Earth to them, while before it would just bleed through, like something coming through the skin."

Our Thoughts and Intentions

Another way the demons can attack from a distance, according to the angels, is simply by focusing their thoughts and intentions on ours to interfere with them. According to the angels, our intentions and thoughts cannot be shielded, and they must be protected through different means. The primary way to block the attacks is by focusing on a single objective, as in meditation. People in the highest state of meditation are absolutely immune to demonic attacks because they literally become a part of the Light (heaven).

Angels suggested another way to ward off the attacks on our thoughts and intentions is by having an intent not to give in to the attacks, not to be possessed or influenced, and to completely reject the works of Satan, his demons, and all the human beings under their influence, and accept the works of God. We can also dedicate our life to God and God's purpose and the purposes we set up in heaven before we came to Earth. When people dedicate their life to God and God's purposes, there is usually constant communication back and forth from God to the person.

All of these suggestions and techniques given by the Light beings through different patients proved to be extremely effective in protecting against different demonic attacks. According to the angels and different Light beings, almost every human being is open for demonic attacks, except maybe a few (.5 percent) who have a special divine purpose and have planned from heaven to have a special bubble round them that totally protects them. They are totally shielded internally and externally.

Shakuntala Modi, M.D.

Invoking God, Masters, and Other Light Beings

Before I begin a session with a patient, I often pray and invoke God, godheads, masters, oversouls, angels, higher self, and heavenly guides of the patient and myself, and everybody whose help we need to protect and guide us. My patients gave the following description of what they saw:

- "As you requested the presence and power of God, godheads, oversouls, masters, archangels, angels, and all the other souls in heaven whose help we need, I see God on the top as brilliant Light, then the godheads, then oversouls under, then all the masters, and the higher selves. I see that masters also have the higher self. They are all wearing white robes, and they all have faces that are changing to help us understand their energy and different identities they have in different religions and different cultures. For example, I see Mother Mary changing into Quanyin and also as Saraswati of the Hindu religion. It seems like a group picture of the hierarchy of heavenly beings. They are all telepathic, even with us.

  "When you asked for the higher self of all the souls to be present, all the people lifted their heads and looked up to be more connected to their higher selves. That was very emotional. I see higher selves as shadowy figures. It knows everything about a person and understands everything. It is a part of our unconscious. It contains all of the knowledge of the soul's past lives and of the whole existence. Higher self has an access to God, masters, oversouls and godheads and can access the knowledge from them about what we need to do. Our higher self has all the knowledge; our soul within does not have all the knowledge.

  "I see oversouls are enormous. It is funny; I feel that they have so much in them that they have to rest. They contain so many lives and so much history in them that they have to sit in chairs. There are multitudes of them, in millions. These are the original souls which were created by God, and as they evolved, they continued to split and live separate lives. Thus, each oversoul now has hundreds of souls living individual lives.

38

That is why they are sitting, because they contain so much information.

"Then I see archangels and angels next to godheads in a separate section for our understanding. It is according to the understanding of their job and purpose.

"I also see different human souls in between the incarnations, in a classroom sitting behind desks and watching everything that we are doing. They are infinite in number.

"Archangel Gabriel is saying that you, Dr. Modi, are chosen as a representative for the whole humanity and when you ask for healing of yourself it will happen for all the humans. So until everybody changes and gets healed, you will hold it."

- "Angels descended from different levels of heaven and came down in streams to go to people and places for which you were praying. I saw people's connecting cords to God opening up throughout the Earth and creation. It was happening on multiple levels of creation that my human mind cannot even conceive. The representation I see is that Light is coming down through people's connecting cords from God, to their hearts. It is like beams of Light coming down that represent connecting cords to God, opening up and becoming stronger and lighter. It was happening on a wider scale throughout creation. It was a blessing of Light and love bestowed upon all beings, which expanded through them and their auras and pushed out their darkness.

  "I saw that more soul parts were coming back to people. This was done a few at a time. As people allowed it to happen and learned from it, more soul parts were brought back. It was a gradual process."

- "When Dr. Modi prayed for all the connections with God to be infused with the golden Light, I saw connecting cords from God to every person and everything in the whole creation, as well as cords going from everybody to all the souls throughout creation. All these connections look like a spider web throughout creation and heaven. I see that we are all connected with everything and everybody throughout the creation and souls in heaven, and then we are all connected to God. I see all the connecting cords throughout the creation filled with the golden Light, which is a richer form of love than the white Light."

- "I see God constantly pouring Light in you and me to protect us and inspire us. As you are working with patients and these demons, God is giving to you and the angels new techniques and ways to transform and deal with the demons, and as a result even angels are evolving. What I am getting is that what you are doing has never been done on this massive scale before, so not only humans, aliens and other souls are evolving in the universe, but the angels and other heavenly beings are also learning and evolving. Vibrations of the planet Earth are steadily rising and are at the critical point, and we cannot go backwards. We have to move ahead.

  "Then when you prayed for the connections between all the dimensions and every soul to be cleansed and healed, I see a big difference in every soul. It is enhancing the healing of every soul and raising their vibrations throughout creation."

- "When Dr. Modi called upon God and masters, I saw the ball of God and masters all around it, as points of Light. They were joined with God, focusing their energy and grace upon us to give us the energy to do whatever we need to do. I saw our higher selves in the Light at the other end of our connecting cord, and beyond that connected to the oversoul and then to God. I saw our guides close to us, and the angels appeared around them. When you called out for the protector angels, it was like ranks and regiments of them were around us, in all dimensions and all directions throughout creation. Four archangels sort of lined up in front of us as if they were ready go to work."

- "It is spectacularly different today. When you first started the prayer, I looked, and instead of seeing God as a personification of the Light, I saw Him as a huge energy being, a glowing ball of intensely brilliant white Light, reaching out and embracing us in His arms. The substance of God penetrated both of us, and we were enveloped in God, and God's energy went through every fiber of us. The incredible warmth and loving energy that

40

came with that was just magnificent. What I am getting is that this is really the normal situation because we are part of God, and this is what we exist in all the time. God is our inner being, and God encompasses the entire universe and is loving and supporting us all the time. We just do not pay attention to it and do not feel it, yet it is always there. It is always ours, supporting, loving, caring, and helping us to follow the path we laid out.

"Instead of seeing angels in Heaven, I saw us sitting here in the office with Archangel Michael at your right hand and Gabriel beside him, Raphael here at my right and Uriel at my left. There are ranks of angels around and all the helpers and watchers are sitting on the side. It was as if the office had been extended and these walls were pushed farther back.

"When you asked for everybody's connecting cord to God to be opened up, I saw the pencil-shaped objects stretching and opening everybody's connecting cords and forcing out the obstruction caused by the dark energy."

Intent to Become a Channel for God, as a Group

One of the suggestions given by heavenly beings is that we can speed the evolution and transformation of ourselves and our planet by becoming an instrument for God's love, Light, power, and healing. According to them, everyone is special to God and can become a tool for His love and healing. He is waiting for us to ask Him to become His instrument, which will help us and other people around us, including those people who are blocked from God by dark influences.

To become a channel for God, first we have to give an intent to become a channel for God. It has to be pure and inspired by love to help others. If we have anger, hate, jealousy, fear, ego, and pride, which are often the result of dark influences, then as a channel we can become blocked by darkness and God cannot work through us. If we feel that for some reason we have become blocked, then we should meditate and pray to be free of these blocks, so we can become a loving person and eventually become a successful channel for God's work.

A minimum of three people are needed to form an intent to become a channel for God. If there are fewer than eight people, we need to hold hands. If there are more than eight, there is no need to hold hands. Then one person in the group can pray for everyone out loud, while others can repeat the prayer silently or out loud. In the prayer, we need to give our intent to become a channel for God's love, Light, power, and healing. This is to benefit everybody forming the intent and all the human beings and to allow us to serve as His instrument as long as our souls exist to overcome the power of Satan, his demons, and humans and other beings under his influence who are working for him.

People who form the intent together remain connected with one another, although they may live far apart. Through their connecting cords to God, they create a wider channel between each other to permit more Light to come through. For example, if three people living in New York, Miami, and Los Angeles form an intent together to become a channel for God and then go to their homes, they, with their connecting cords to God, create a triangle between them. Together they create a wider channel, and more intense Light can come through the triangle to help all those around them, and between them. Most of the Light is where the channels are, but people who are geographically encompassed between the channels get filled with the Light of God as well.

When we dedicate our life individually to God, it is an individual act and is beneficial to ourselves only. Forming a channel for God as a group is beneficial to all who are in the group, and it spreads to other people around them and between them. It is a group act. Here, God is the main actor and director. Following is the prayer that can be used to form an intent to become a channel for God:

"Dear God, please permit us to serve as a channel for your love, Light, power, and healing for the benefit of ourselves and for all human beings and the planet. Allow us to serve as your instrument to overcome the power of Satan, his demons, and those human and alien beings who serve Him. We seek to do this as long as our soul shall exist. Thank you."

During a conference, when I prayed for the whole group to become a "channel for God" and also said the protection prayer, one of the attendees gave the following description of what she observed during the prayer.

• "When Dr. Modi spoke about the protection prayers, I saw bolts and shafts of white and golden Light enter individuals' heads. The Light seemed to spread from one individual to another, making a connection of Light and forming a dome over all individuals in the room. Many balls of Light that were coming from heaven then took the forms of angels and others. I saw Archangels Metatron, Michael, Raphael, and Gabriel, along with other angels of Light, over the heads of the individuals seated. Many of the individuals had the same angel, archangel, and/or master. There were many forms of individuals that I could not recognize. As Dr. Modi continued with her prayer, more and more Light entered the room.

"I could see many dark forms leaving the bodies of individuals, and at the same time, see white Light enter the same body. A lot of conversations were going on, sounding almost confusing. It seemed like all Light beings were talking at the same time to their Earthly being, yet everyone they were speaking to did not seem confused. The dome of the Light looked like layers of very fine netting connecting all who were under it."

Triple Net of Light and Metallic Shield

While working with patients, sometimes it was hard to keep the human, demon, and other spirits out of the patients because their aura was weak and their physical and emotional conditions were making them vulnerable to infestation by the outside spirits. So heavenly beings suggested putting the triple net of Light and metallic shield around these people and the spirits would have a hard time intruding and affecting them. The Heavenly beings said I should place these shields only when needed and remove them when not needed because they block the telepathic communication (which we are not even aware of) with a large number of people. One of the patients gave the following description.

- "I saw Light coming down through the connecting cords of people, all through the different levels of this building, and filling it. Everybody's aura was expanding, and they were shielded with a triple net of Light, metallic shield, and mirror shield. As you asked for protection of this room in your office, the angels put a large glass sheet, except it was like a transparent bluish crystal, which is designed to protect and shield you from the dark influences from the outside. I saw a circle of angels standing facing outward to guard. The walls around the office also exist on the spiritual level but not the roof, which permits the Light to pour into the room."

Dark Centers

My patients under hypnosis sometimes described seeing dark centers in the space from where the demons try to interfere during the sessions. They appear like black spaceships or huge black blobs and are invisible to most people. Only psychics or people under hypnosis can see them. Inside these centers are computer like equipment and devices, and demons are observing, controlling and manipulating people from there. People see black cords coming out of these dark centers and going to different people. These demons have soul parts of all the people in the area controlled by that dark command center, and they feed different thoughts to an individual or a group of people to cause them problems.

These demons claim to broadcast negative thoughts to all the people through their soul parts and their connecting cords, which are in the demon's possession. This affects their feelings, and then their behavior follows. They sprinkle a dust of dark energy and cover the whole planet and everything and everybody in it. People do not know it is there. The demons create negative thoughts in one religion against the other, one country against the other, and one person against the other. They also can insert or block things in people.

These demons claimed to have dark command centers all over creation. I asked angels to collect all the demons from the dark centers, transform them, and take them to heaven. Dissolve all the dark centers, transform them into the Light, and take the energy to heaven. I asked the angels to collect all the soul parts of people from the dark centers, cleanse them, heal them, cut their dark connections, and take them back to whom they belong and integrate them after cleansing and healing completely. Over the past twenty-four years, we located and transformed most of the dark centers and the factories where they were created from all over creation. We also transformed all the planetary commanders, the top commander for the whole creation, and trillions of demons who were working under them and sent them to heaven. They still are able to create a few dark centers with great difficulty. So we still need to continue to pray to dissolve and transform them and take the energy to heaven.

- "When you asked for the dark command centers to be covered with the blanket of Light and dissolve them, I saw thousands of protector angels going to different dark centers all over creation, covering them with the blanket of Light and transforming the dark centers totally into the Light, and taking them to heaven.

  "When you asked that the dark centers in hell be destroyed, Satan filed his protest that Light cannot do that because it will be breaking the rules. God pointed out, 'Yes, partly Satan is right that he has to have his own space, and what he does inside his space is his business. It is when he infringes outside through his dark centers, then they get destroyed.'"

- "There are few dark command centers left since you have been dissolving and transforming them. They are larger and the connecting tubes are really thick, almost as thick as the centers, with their connections going straight from those tubes down to different people and places. It is like Satan is running out of places to put them. I saw connections between demons being cut, soul parts of people being picked up and cleansed and taken to those to whom they belong and integrated after cleansing them. I saw this happening in multiple dimensions."

Light Centers

One of my patients under hypnosis told me there is a Light center around my office building. She was given the understanding that I created this Light center while I went to heaven during my sleep at night. I was completely surprised to hear that because I had no conscious knowledge of it. She described it as being made up of white crystalline Light surrounding the whole building and around the individual offices, and she saw different heavenly beings helping us from there.

I asked God through the hypnotized patient if we can create these Light centers around every dimension, home, building, and car throughout creation, and God said, "Ask and it will be done." So I prayed to God and requested the angels to create the Light centers around the whole creation and around every dimension, every home, building, transportation vehicle, water body, forest, street, and land. I also requested Light centers around every room and hallway; this way the angels can guard and protect every room and hallway and heavenly guides can guide us. It was done.

Before, I had been advised by heavenly beings to use triple net of Light and metallic shield only when needed because they interfere with the telepathic communication with large numbers of people. Now with the Light centers being created all over the Earth and creation, information and the Light can be sent directly through them, and there is much less darkness to interfere. There was a sense of great love and joy coming from God and heavenly beings as these Light centers were created. My hypnotized patients gave the following descriptions:

- "It all feels like one piece of glass made up of crystalline Light, and it is about a foot thick. It is very high and is all around the building, including at the bottom covering the vortexes. The top of the Light center is in a dome shape. As I look inside the Light center, I see some angelic forms with wings, inside. They are transparent and are moving around. There are also beings without wings; I think they are our heavenly guides. There are several cords going from the Light center to heaven. I see there are sections in the Light center for each apartment. As I see different homes in the neighborhood, I see individual Light centers for each home, and there is one larger above, covering the Light centers above several homes.

"When I look at my apartment, I see it covered with a Light center. Actually, every apartment has its own center inside the big Light center, like my apartment, including top, sides, and the floor, seemed to be wrapped in a smaller Light center. As I look in my bedroom, I see an extension from the Light center above my bed like a showerhead, and each hole in it has Light streaming. I also see another showerhead type of device above my computer in my bedroom. These showerheads or strainers have extensions like flexible tubes like spaghetti. They are like strings of Light or tentacles of Light, about six to eight in each showerhead. They are balancing the energy in space and become very specific. I see angels are watching and guiding me through these showerhead type of devices."

- "When you asked the Light centers to be built in place of the dark centers around every universe, galaxy, solar system, planetary system, sun, moon, star, and dimension, including all around the Earth, around every nation, state, county, town and city, every building, and every room in each building, I saw angels creating these concentric centers of Light all over the creation. I heard God saying, 'Thank you. I have been waiting for centuries for somebody from the universe to ask for it, but before now nobody thought of asking for it.' I also heard Satan protesting to God and saying it is not fair, and God is telling him that we have a right to ask for protection and it will be provided.

  "When you asked for all the homes and buildings to be enclosed in the Light center, Satan protested again that this absolutely not happen. Angels did it, but they had to let God decide whether it was fair or not. Satan protested that we cannot set it up in such a way that they cannot get to people. God said that Satan does have a right to approach people, but those who want the protection will have it.

"I saw Light centers being created all around the schools, universities, nursing homes, hospitals, prison buildings, and all the buildings on Earth and creation, including everybody's homes, workplaces, and every room in them. They were almost getting in each other's way."

• "I saw extensions of God with his big arms around us and I felt that warm loving feeling again. I saw Light centers around each building and each room, overlapping each other. They also put the triple net of Light around the Light centers. Before it was important to communicate telepathically with the large number of people, but the triple net of Light would interfere with the information coming through in large quantities. It was easier and efficient to broadcast to everybody in the universe at the same time. Now because of the Light centers being created everywhere, information and Light can be sent directly through them, and there is less darkness to interfere."

Vortexes

Over the years, my hypnotized patients often reported that most of the churches, temples, mosques, and other places of worship are built on the energy vortexes. Also there are many vortexes in and around the Earth. Normally, vortexes are filled with Light. They create a kind of compression chamber on the planet. They create positive energy, and the healing work is accelerated, and people around them can open up psychically; these are the power places.

Over the years, the demons have infested the Light vortexes and made them dark and negative. They create dark vortexes next to the Light vortex and over time contaminate them, making them dark, affecting people negatively. People under hypnosis see that these vortexes are connected to and influence each other. Also, what people living around those vortexes do affects the vortexes. If they are involved with negative and evil actions, they create negative energy with low vibrations, and the vortexes there become dark, while the good actions will increase the Light and vibrations of the vortexes.

I requested the angels to cleanse and remove all the dark and other entities, energies, and dark devices, and heal all the existing natural and dark vortexes. Cleanse them, heal them, and transform them into the Light and take them to heaven. Remove all the soul parts of people from all the vortexes, including the dark vortexes; cleanse them, heal them, fill them with the Light, and integrate them where they belong. Then I prayed to God to flood all the vortexes with the crystalline Light and shield them with the triple compression chamber of crystalline Light, and place mirror shields and rays of white Light at both ends of the vortexes and the inner and outer walls.

I heard about the vortex of Sedona, Arizona, which is considered to be a power place. Many people reported changes in themselves when they visited. They claim to have become more spiritual and psychic, so I asked one patient under hypnosis to look at the vortex in Sedona and find out what makes it so powerful. She saw tiny crystals all over the vortex that increased the vibrations of energy in the vortex.

Some patients under hypnosis also reported that by creating the crop circles in the fields, aliens in some cases were creating vortexes underneath. Some patients under hypnosis also reported that there are no natural vortexes under the pyramids in Egypt, so the basement or underground parts of some of the pyramids were created in a way to create a vortex effect.

I began to wonder if we could create the vortexes under all homes, buildings, structures, farm lands, water bodies, forests, mountains, and all the land on Earth, and all around the Earth and creation. Then these can raise the vibrations of the whole planet, creation, and everybody in it. So again, I asked God through the hypnotized patient if we can do that, and the answer was, "Yes! Ask and it will be done, but ask only for Earth. It is not yet time for other planets in the creation."

So I prayed to God to create vortexes all around the Earth and all over the Earth: under all the homes, buildings, structures, water bodies, mountains, forests, farms, and all the land. The patient saw the vortexes being created instantly, almost like magic. I also prayed to put tiny crystals in all the created and natural vortexes, and then

I requested the angels to shield the vortexes all over and around the Earth at the top and the bottom end and inside and outside of the sides with a triple compression chamber of crystalline Light, mirror shields, and rays of white crystalline Light. I also requested the angels to create a grid of Light over all the created and natural vortexes to protect them from the demons, and it was done.

We were given the understanding that the Light comes from above from God and from below the vortexes. Sunlight also activates the crystals, so God and sunlight work together. Because of these vortexes, vibrations will be raised in all the homes and the people who live there and all over the planet Earth. People will become more energized, positive, spiritual, and closer to God.

According to the heavenly beings, during the transition to the fifth dimension, all these vortexes will help in uplifting the planet.

- "I see the vortex under our building and all of New York City as black and red. Inside the vortex, it looks like burning reddish coal, but it is transparent, because it is not coal. Inside of the vortex, it is pale gray. The vortex under our building is the size of the building and the land around it. There is a large vortex stretching throughout the street. Every street has its own dark vortexes that are grayish in color. There is one for each block number on the avenue. Some of them go beyond the streets. I see a big vortex for the whole island of Manhattan, which is grayish. All the vortexes were cleansed, healed, and filled with the crystalline Light and shielded with triple compression chambers of the crystalline Light, inside, and also outside on your request. Angels also put tiny crystals inside the vortexes to raise the vibrations of them and everything around them."

- "God is sending a powerful Light to all land and ocean vortexes. I see a transparent shield all around the earth, around the opening of the earth on both ends (connecting cords of the earth). Light beams are put on all individual vortexes around the earth. All the vortexes all over the earth opened up and activated, it appears as if the Light is transcending all over the creation and connecting cords of all the souls are opening up.

I see Light illuminating all over the earth, every cell of every organism that is also a vortex, and more energy is coming to everyone. The vortex in each and every being is activated and opened and energy is permeating through each of them. During the transition to the fifth dimension, all these vortex activations will help in up lifting the planet."

A few months after we created vortexes under every home and building, I began to feel sleepy at certain spot on the street while driving home from the office. My eyes would close for a few seconds, and I was scared that I would have an accident. It was so bad that I was afraid that I might have to stop driving. I just had an intuitive feeling that some demons were trying to influence me. So during a session I asked a person under hypnosis to check and see what was going on at that spot on the street. She was instantly shown a couple of demons sitting on a tree, using a laser beam type of device to make me sleepy. I prayed to God and requested the angels to surround the demons in the net of Light. Following is a transcript of the conversation:

DR. MODI: Dark one why are you interfering with me?

DEMON: (Angry) Since you created the vortexes under every home and building, we cannot go there to interfere with people. We cannot tolerate the higher vibrations there (laughing). But you forgot to create these vortexes under the streets, and we can influence people from here. We make people impatient and angry while driving, sometimes leading to killing. We make people tired and sleepy, thus causing the accidents and some-times death. We wanted to get rid of you by killing you while driving. We do not want you to write your books and tell people about us and how to get rid of us.

DR. MODI: We pray to God and request the angels to please col-lect in the nets of Light these and all the other demons who are assigned to cause problems on the streets and highways throughout the earth. Cut their dark connections with Satan, his demons, people, and places, transform them into the Light and take them to heaven please.

PATIENT: I see all the demons changing into the Light and going to heaven with the angels.

DR. MODI: We pray to God and request the angels to please create the vortexes under all the highways and streets, under all the lands including the farmlands, water bodies, mountains, and everywhere we need to create one.

PATIENT: I see vortexes are created everywhere instantly.

DR. MODI: Please shield all the vortexes with the triple compression chamber of crystalline Light inside and outside and also at the lower and upper end. Put tiny crystals inside the vortexes. Then put a grid net over all the vortexes to prevent any demonic invasion.

PATIENT: I see all this happening all over the earth like magic.

DR. MODI: We thank God for creating these vortexes all over the earth. Thank you from the bottom of our hearts for the wonderful gift.

Violet Flame

According to heavenly beings, one of the most awesome gifts given by the grace of God to every human being who desires it, and to our planet at this time, is the "violet flame." It has the power and potential to heal and transform us, our planet, and even the whole universe. If we can visualize the white Light of God under a prism, we can see the seven colors of a rainbow. Each color has a different vibration, quality, and function. The violet color has the highest vibration and the power to transmute and transform the negative energies and entities. It is described by my patients as the "flame of mercy," "flame of freedom," "flame of forgiveness," "flame of love of God," "flame of transmutation," "flame of transformation," "a fountain of youth," "antidote for negative energy and disease," "flame of the grace of God," and so forth.

According to the heavenly beings, violet flame can transmute and transform the dark entities, dark shields, dark devices, dark blocks, and dark energies from inside and around us. Gradually, it can absorb and dissipate all our negative thoughts and feelings—that is, anger, hate, jealousy, pride, ego, and arrogance, and it can eradicate all the violent and negative behavior. It can heal our emotional, mental, and physical problems. It can dissolve all the karmic imprints from our DNA and from our planet, and thus free us from our personal and planetary karmas (actions) from this life and from all the other lifetimes from the beginning of time, and it can purify us and our planet. It has the potential to reverse the aging process and conquer death. Then we would not have to die from disease or old age, which are often the result of karma. We can live as long as we want to, and we can choose to leave the planet, still looking young and healthy, when our work here is done.

Violet flame can also ward off the planetary upheavals, earth changes, and all the future predictions of nuclear cataclysm and Armageddon between Light and dark. We can raise the vibrations of ourselves and our planet and become closer to the Light and God. We can live and function as pure Light beings, free of any and all dark influences. Violet flame is God's love, grace, power, and healing in action.

According to heavenly beings, God has promised to dispense this astounding power of violet flame to transform the human race, Earth and the whole universe, but we must exert our free will and ask for it—not just a few people or a few spiritual groups here and there, but each and every person regardless of who he or she is. It does not matter who we are and what we have done; this gift is given to all without discrimination. Just ask for the violet flame and watch it create miracles for our planet, the whole universe, and us. It has unlimited potential. Angels often suggested asking for the violet fire to be infused after cleansing and healing of people and places.

It is a golden opportunity given to us by the love and grace of God. For some, it can be a one-way ticket to eternal life. We can enter into the golden age free of all the dark influences and ills of our society. All we have to do is pray and ask for it, and God will do the rest.

Imagine a violet liquid fire, similar to lava, pouring from God like a waterfall through the silver connecting cords to all the dimensions throughout the creation and everything and everybody in creation and all around it, including the whole Earth and around it. This includes each and every human being, other living beings, and their surroundings, blazing into intense flames and dissolving and dissipating all the negative entities, energies, thoughts, feelings, relationships, and daily problems and behaviors. It gradually transforms the whole Earth and all the human and living beings on it.

Picture a globe of Earth dipped into and filled with violet liquid fire that is blazing into intense violet flame, nonstop, twenty-four hours a day. If there is some part of Earth facing special problems like war, disaster, or famine, then focus on those areas and fill them with the concentrated violet liquid fire and violet flames for a longer time, several times a day until the problem is resolved.

Then imagine violet liquid fire pouring like violet lava from God through your connecting silver cord in and around you like a waterfall, penetrating and permeating your mind, soul, and every part, every organ, every cell and strand of DNA of your body, and igniting into intense violet flames, spreading in and around you, all through your home, workplaces, cars, and everything and everybody in them and miles and miles around nonstop, twenty-four-hours a day.

You can also invoke the violet flame for your family members, friends, coworkers, people who did harm to you, people whom you harmed, and even your enemies. Anybody and anything you choose can be put in that violet fire, including your day-to-day problems and issues and all your physical, emotional, mental, and relationship problems, and they can be resolved and transformed. Imagine that violet liquid fire pouring continuously and blazing into intense flames, nonstop, twenty-four hours a day.

You can also imagine your body made up of transparent crystal, and through it you can clearly see every part and organ in your body. Then visualize that violet liquid fire coming from God through your connecting cord and going through your whole body. As this liquid fire penetrates and permeates through every part, every organ, every cell, and every strand of DNA, it ignites into flames, blazing through your mind, body, soul, connecting cord, energy field, and surroundings. Imagine all the dark energies, entities and problems in the body being transformed, thus healing your mind, body and soul. Following are some of the descriptions about the violet flame given by my hypnotized patients.

- "When Dr. Modi asked for the violet liquid fire, I saw the waves of violet liquid fire flowing through the whole creation like a tide, filling everything and everybody and blazing into flames all the time. As I look at myself, it is blazing in me and all around me, too."

- "When Dr. Modi prayed for the violet flame to transform the relationships, negative emotions, and physical problems, I saw what looked like a design in the computer chip inside the cell and little angels making changes in the connections there. It was a very complex pattern with all sorts of crossover, little spots and bars with different devices on them. The tiny angels were just moving a connection from here to there or establishing new connections and bridging over the top. What I think they were doing is changing the karmic imprints from the DNA."

- "When Dr. Modi asked for the Earth to be dipped into the violet flame, I saw, like in cooking, Earth being dipped into the violet liquid fire and blazing into flames. It was kind of soaked into it."

- "When Dr. Modi prayed for violet fire, I saw beautiful violet fire all over the creation which was kind of transparent, so you can see through it. It is not heavy and it is moving all the time because fire is in motion. Fire is like the conversation with the space. So depending on the changes in the space it moves around, curving up and down."

New Techniques for Speedy Healing

Most of the techniques given by God so far are powerful and effective in cleansing, healing, shielding, and protecting us, but according to archangels, now we need even faster healing because of what is going to happen in the future. During this time, Earth, sun, and the center of the galaxy are going to align with each other and planet Earth and all humanities will have a chance to shift from the third dimension, where we are now, to the fifth dimension, which will be like living in heaven to some extent. There will be no demonic influence; that means there will be no pain, suffering, sickness, or aging. We will not die because of disease, aging, or some outside force. We will choose to leave the body voluntarily when our purpose is fulfilled.

Everybody has to make a conscious decision whether they want to move into the fifth dimension or not. If they choose not to move into the fifth dimension, then they will be given another third dimension planet and live under similar conditions to how we are living now for about the next 26,000 years. But if they choose to move into the fifth dimension, they will have to be free of all the demonic influences and get back all their soul parts, which they have lost in thousands of past lives and the current life; otherwise Satan will hold them back with those soul parts and the connecting cords to their soul.

According to heavenly beings, all human beings have lived thousands of past lives, during which they lost millions and trillions of soul parts which are in the possession of Satan and his demons, as well as with people, places, darkness, and heaven, and everybody has layers and layers of dark entities and energies in them.

Heavenly beings said that even though the techniques given by God so far to remove all the entities and energies and bring back the missing soul parts are very effective, we still will not succeed with it. So now, with the grace and love of God, we are given the following techniques, allowing everybody to heal faster and completely, regardless of who we are and what we have done. But everybody has to make a conscious choice to move into the fifth dimension. We need to use these amazing techniques daily and pray for complete healing.

Crystalline Light

During a session, angels used crystalline, white Light for cleansing and healing, instead of the regular white Light they were using before. They claimed that crystalline Light was more powerful and effective during the healing, and God is now allowing us to use it.

Triple Compression Chamber of Crystalline Light

During a session with a patient under hypnosis, a very black ball of Satan's soul part was pushed out of her by a powerful Light coming from God on my request. This soul part was extremely strong and belonged to Satan's core. It was so powerful that even angels were afraid to go close enough to put a net of Light around it. So I prayed to God to provide new techniques to work with Satan and his demons. As a result, God put a compression chamber around that powerful soul part of Satan, and it was taken to heaven. The angels did not have to go close to it or touch it.

The patient described this compression chamber as a gelatin capsule. The waves of Light were going into the darkness and the particles were surrounding it. It was not a laser Light, which is a concentrated beam, but the compression chamber has a heavy saturation of Light, which immobilizes the demons. They cannot even fight against the Light; they get transformed whether they like it or not. It has a transparent crystal shield, so the angels can see the demons inside and supervise them but do not have to touch them. Angels and heavenly beings have special protective shields around them and are immune to demonic influences; they have extra fortification and wisdom. They also have a device like a sword of Light to cut the dark connections, similar to laser Light.

Later on, it was changed into a triple compression chamber of crystalline Light, which is even more powerful than the single compression chamber of crystalline Light. Patients describe it as a flexible round or oval-shaped container. There are no sharp corners, and three bands of crystalline Light hold in the walls of the chamber between them. There are more flexible wires or veins. It looks like a fabric that can bellow out. Nothing can get in or out unless we put something in or remove it. The pressure inside squeezes all the air out of whatever is inside of it. It compacts the life force inside.

The size of the triple compression chamber depends on what is inside. It has a lid on the top to see what is happening inside. We can put an intention in the crystalline bands that anything entering that is not needed is cleansed, healed, and removed automatically. These shields cannot be penetrated except from the other dimensions of the same vibrations. Entities can come in from one dimension to the other through the inter- and intra-dimensional pathways.

Again, I asked God if we can put the triple compression chamber of crystalline Light around the whole creation and everything and everybody in the creation. He said to ask, and as soon as I did, they were everywhere instantly throughout the creation. They were around all the dimensions, homes, buildings, and all the rooms and hallways in them, around yards, vortexes underneath, roads, water bodies, farmlands, forests, mountains, and around all the humans, animals, trees, plants and all the creatures and souls. My patients gave the following descriptions about the triple compression chamber of Light.

- "I see the soul part of Satan in heaven in a compression chamber, which was taken out of me a couple of days ago. It required many, many angels to do that. Even in the compression chamber, it is changing very slowly. It seems to be very condensed, black, and powerful. There are multitudes of soul parts of me and other people, which are brought out of this soul part of Satan when you asked for it. I see a screen or a filter on one side of the compression chamber and all the soul parts are coming out of it, but soul parts of Satan are staying in. They cannot come out of it yet. The angels have set up a big compression chamber in heaven and put all the soul parts of Satan in it which you released from every soul all over the creation."

- "I am seeing a compression chamber near the healing clinics in heaven for the damaged soul parts of people, so they can be worked on and healed. It is like there is a phase one, phase two, and phase three for healing. Phase one is the compression, cleaning, and healing of the damaged soul parts; phase two is the healing clinic where they rest and heal; and phase three is the release and return to where they belong. These compression chambers are new devices. They were not there before and are given by God because you have been praying for faster ways of working with demons, transforming them and healing people."

Activating and Healing the Self-Healing Strand of DNA

One of the fast-healing techniques God allowed during the end of 2009 was to activate the self-healing strand of DNA, so the body can heal itself as it was supposed to. Heavenly beings through my hypnotized patients mentioned that our DNA has thirty-two strands, but except for two strands, the rest of them were blocked off from the beginning, including the self-healing strand of DNA. Although there was always some minor self-healing going on, such as scab formation on a wound, most was prevented by blocking the self-healing strand, so there was no Light going through it. When I prayed for faster techniques for our healing, the archangels said that God is allowing the cleansing and healing of the self-healing strand of DNA, and as a result, there will be an automatic healing of our mind, body, and soul from the beginning of our incarnation as a human being. Healing of DNA will also be allowed for all the dimensions and other beings throughout the creation.

So I prayed to God to send the Lightning bolts of crystalline Light through the self-healing strands of DNA and cleanse, heal, and activate them, and speed up the self-healing process. It would have happened naturally if it was not blocked off at the beginning. The original process was set up to expand as it grew because expansion is the normal process that was designed for growth. When it was slowed down, the normal process became the aging process, which led to death. Now with the activation and healing of the self-healing strand of DNA, it will cause the reversal of the aging process. Following are some of the descriptions my hypnotized patients gave about what they saw when I prayed.

- "When Dr. Modi prayed to put the magnetic sheet around the self-healing strand of the DNA and send the Lightning bolts through the self-healing strands of DNA to reverse the blockage, the Light came inside it, and it lit up. I also see it speeding up as she asked for it. The original self-healing process has slowed down from eons of time. So when she asked for the Lightning bolt to go through that strand of self-healing, it just lighted up. There has been some self-healing all along with scabs forming on wounds, but the Light was not strong enough. Then when she asked for the instructions to be changed, they were changed up to the present; they did not go all the way up to the past. It needs to be upgraded from the beginning when the original instruction was sent to slow down the healing process to the minimum. It is also good because it has the designed effect. It is never a straight line; it has a quality to become a vortex.

  "What I am seeing is that there are thirty-two strands of DNA, but except for two strands, all of them were blocked off from the beginning. I see the self-healing strand of DNA as a tube that has instructions with the dark lines in them because it was not operating anymore. It was not self-healing. When Dr. Modi prayed to God to send the bolts of crystalline Light through the self-healing DNA strand of everybody and speed up the natural process of self-healing of the body, I see bolts of crystalline Light coming from the hand of God. It is a crystalline, faceted energy, shooting through every self-healing strand of DNA of every dimension and every soul. It is going through the tubes of history that were dormant in all humanity and all the other bodies and dimensions throughout the creation. The Lightning bolt is shooting through to activate that one strand of DNA of all the bodies and dimensions throughout the creation, whose function is to maintain the self-healing properties. The Light is shooting through to activate and to remember its original purpose, which was set up to expand as it grew, that was designed for growth. When it was slowed down, the normal process became the aging process and led to death, an involuntary death. This speeding up will be self-healing inside that expands as the healing progresses. There is a time element to accumulation of wisdom that goes with the capacity of the body to be fully in charge of itself and in full control, not weakened by varying diseases and aging process."

- "As Dr. Modi asked God to send the Lightning bolt through the self-healing strand of DNA, I am seeing it light up and expand, and these strands are waking up to what their job is. As I look at myself, I see an opening up of the self-healing strand, like little baby eyes that were sleeping are opening up. When they are fully activated, they will function better.

  "When you focus on the aging process, there are various channels within the body that have historical information that needs to be balanced and liberated, so they can function more flexibly. The channels come from the original patterns of the humans at the time the current aging process was designed as a method for humans to go through different experiences. These are like threads or tubes that go all over the body. Each human has them, and they connect to other humans. It is part of the common beliefs that holds together the human form, the variations within pretty small limitations of humans and the belief. At this time, all humans are connecting to this concept that the body heals itself. The concept of healing itself involves the possibility of age reversal at various speeds. It is part of this common experience that is being brought together by paying

61

attention now to these channels, so that the greater acceleration can be affected. These channels are not meridians, etheric nadis, or kundalini; they are kind of a grid system, which goes from one human to the other. To reverse the aging process, you can look at what is there, and if there is any blockage in the belief system you can remove it by putting the magnetic sheet around it."

- "When Dr. Modi asked for healing of the self-healing strand of DNA for the whole creation and to implement the original instruction for self-healing, I saw it going in historically to change the genetic history of humanity, so that the current bodies that are alive in the present year of 2009 would benefit from self-healing. It has been coming from the beginning of time to change the energy in their ancestors, so the genetic development would happen. As I look at it, it is progressing geometrically, but it still is pretty slow, and we will not see the results immediately.

    "The interferences to other parts of creation are not as extreme as the interference in the beings such as the humans, aliens, and animals. There is a relationship in consciousness that permits greater change, which will be coming along as we move in time, because this energy is moving in time. It is not just inside of this time, but it is also outside of time. There is always a portion of everything that is in time; it is also outside the time, like the elementals are in time and are also outside the time.

    "All humans that are on Earth at this time have had some connection with a lifetime that was partially physical and partially etheric. That particular genetic memory needs to be activated in order to speed up the progress of this particular DNA strand, which is connected to the consciousness. A consciousness is of the Light. A consciousness of relationship of humanity to all of nature needs to be activated in all the humans because the rest of nature in creation has a better connection to its original plans than the humans with the interference that has existed.

"Many people have had this consciousness all along, which was maintained in the overall consciousness of humanity. So these have been lifted, but the memory—the habit—is still there, which needs to be changed. The changes will occur as all humanity has an expanded feeling when they wake up that they are part of sky, trees, animals, the birds, and the insects. Ask to expand the Light of consciousness within humanity, so they know that they are part of the whole creation."

• "When you prayed to send the Lightning bolts through the self-healing strands of DNA, and remove everything that does not belong and expand the consciousness of the whole humanity, there was a consciousness of multidimensionality when people become conscious of their participation with nature, because nature is more multidimensional in its perfected understanding of itself than humans who separated themselves out. What I saw was Lightning bolts going through the self-healing strand, and it got wider and even expanded on the sides. Then when you activated the memory that started to happen like a tiny seed, because it has gone for a very long time. Memory is there, but it has to be brought from the original human body to the current human body, and there have been billions and trillions of human bodies since the original one."

• "When Dr. Modi prayed to activate the memory of the self-healing strand of DNA, from the beginning of its existence from the original body, through all the bodies of all the incarnations it has taken, and cleanse and heal the memories of all the negativity and the darkness, which has obscured them, by sending the Lightning bolt through this self-healing strand of DNA from lifetime to lifetime and activating the memories and awareness of its purpose completely, I saw like a cloud of black coal dust which was all being taken away and the memory became a bright, white, dancing Light within each human who is here now on this planet Earth. It is done only for the humans, and they will become aware of their purpose in response to this healing.

63

"When you thanked God on behalf of the whole creation for this gift of self-healing, I heard Him thanking us for being Him and understanding these parts of healing."

- "As I look at you, Dr. Modi, you have all these golden lines coming out of your arms, chest, back, and head and all the upper part of your body, including the heart. They are golden threads, like thin hair, going up to the Light. These are the feeding tubes you have between you and heaven to receive the information from all the dimensions. It looks like a halo, but is composed of all these strings of different qualities, like different strands of DNA, which contain instructions. It is almost as if you are a factory, and there are openings on the top, and people who are working there are pouring different ingredients in each one of these, such as different ideas, different thoughts, different creations, different patterns, and different rules. All these are very subtle; it is a heavenly organization. There is a precise combination in each movement in time. These strings are also connected to the Akashic records.

  "Your higher self is saying these strings coming out of you were always there, but now they are activated. As they are further activated, they will get bigger, and more information and the knowledge will come to you. These strings are straight; they do not curve. You have been using them but did not realize it. It is related to the largeness. The enormity of your work is hard for you to grasp right now."

Changing the Regular DNA into Crystalline DNA

I read somewhere that we can pray for our DNA to be changed into crystalline DNA, so during one session I prayed for the regular DNA to be activated into crystalline DNA for every dimension and soul, and the patient saw all the thirty-two strands of DNA changing into crystalline DNA. It will raise the vibrations of the humans and other beings. The patient gave the following description.

- "When you asked all the thirty-two strands of DNA to be activated into crystalline DNA, I saw all the thirty-two strands of DNA made up of crystalline Light. They were open in the middle, like a tube, and the crystalline Light was put in them to activate them, and they will be operational when the time is right. They are activated on the etheric level. There are layers of activation at different levels of our consciousness and the union of our own spiritual evolution. I see about twelve to fifteen strands of your DNA are activated. They have a different color and look more solid; other DNA strands are fainter."

Activation of the DNA of the Body and Soul

- "As Dr. Modi prayed to God to activate the DNA of all the dimensions, humans, aliens, and other beings' bodies and souls throughout the creation, I see energy rising in the core of the Earth and also see a glow in the base chakra of every person. In most people, the glow is just staying there, but in some people it is slightly higher up. This is the DNA of kundalini energy, which is activated for the Earth and all the dimensions through-out the creation and their people and other souls who live on those dimensions. The glow appears as silver, gold sparkles, like glitter in liquid Light, shaken up. There is a kinetic energy in it. I see that kundalini and the soul DNA are the same but not exactly the same. They are intertwined and connected somehow. I see my Kundalini energy moving up and down up to my sexual chakra while yours is going above the belly button chakra. I see it happening throughout the creation. It is as though a switch has been turned on, and the energy is rising for all beings throughout the creation with spiritual practices. This is the part of the movement to a higher vibration throughout the Earth and creation."

Activation

- "When you prayed for activation of mind, body and soul, all thirty-two strands of DNA including the self-healing strand, the Kundalini, meridians, nadis, chakras, psychic antennas, physical, emotional, mental, and spiritual bodies, connecting cords to God, masters, higher self, guides and angels, and Akashic records for every being and every dimension throughout the creation, I saw golden Light pouring like thick lava and gently stretching all the tubes. It was full of love and joy. When you asked for magnetic sheets to be activated it was activated the first time you placed the magnetic sheets and then it becomes stronger every time you ask it to be activated.

"Archangel Gabriel is saying that when you activate a strand of DNA, kundalini, meridian, nadis, and chakras, it makes it easier for the flow of energy to go through every part of the body and the brain and clear up that part. It is about clarity and that every part is functioning better. Continue to ask for the activation of every part, every cord, and every channel regularly, because there are many layers of history that people have and the healing happens a layer at a time. It is like the fine line of energy opening up like another stream. It clears out various parts that people will eventually attract to themselves where there is more Light. It is all about people attracting the familiar darkness towards them, even though there is not much darkness left anymore.

"You can continue to ask for the activation of thirty-two strands of DNA, and when people are ready, it will be activated for every soul. So far, besides the two regular strands of DNA, the self-healing strand of DNA is activated. You can activate all the golden cords, which are coming out of the upper part of your body and going to heaven, and ask them to be infused with the golden liquid Light, making them larger. Each cord is an original plan about how that part needs to function—the part where it is attached but also to much more than just the part.

"When you prayed for all the golden cords to be activated and opened up more, I saw golden liquid Light like olive oil being poured in. It pushed the cords back and made them wider. Also the knowledge, wisdom and gifts are poured through them."

Magnetic Sheet

One of the techniques given to us through the love and grace of God is the magnetic sheet. According to my hypnotized patients, the magnetic sheet looks like a covering of shimmering Light. It is like a crystalline Light, but it is not transparent. It is more akin to matter; it covers the whole body and every part and organ inside. Once it is there it becomes the magnet, then it sends a tone of itself out of the magnetic ray. In electromagnets, the electric part is the lightning, and magnetic part is the magnet pulling in. So here you can see duality: one aspect comes in and the other goes out.

The magnetic sheet is the connection on a spiritual physical level. It can go over, under, and inside everything. It is a level of attraction. It will attract to itself what is required. It is flexible, very thin, and strong. It molds and adapts to anything like saran wrap and will attract the Light (soul parts). It is continuous and soft. Usually there is one magnetic sheet, but it has layers within it, even though we cannot see them. It maintains its own magnetic absolute. It is powerful and does not dissipate in any way. We can command it to go wherever we want it to go. It will act the same way whether it is small or large. It is not heavy and can cut through anything. It goes where it needs to without interfering with anything. It is similar to how radio waves or cell phones work: We do not see them, but they are there.

Once we place magnetic sheets and the triple compression chamber of crystalline Light, people cannot reject them. Although the technique is very fast, the healing is still happening slowly for everybody; otherwise our bodies would explode with all those soul parts coming in.

Archangel Michael suggested asking the angels to create a switch on all the magnetic sheets. On one side is written "Eject" and on the other side is written "Attract." In the prayers, we can request the angels to turn the switch of all the magnetic sheets to the Eject sign, and they will eject everything that does not belong there. Then we can ask the angels to collect in the net of Light whatever is ejected, transform them into the Light, and take it to the

Heaven. Then we can pray to God to flood the whole creation and everything and everybody in it with the white, crystalline, liquid Light and remove whatever is left.

Then we can ask the angels to turn the switch of the magnetic sheets to the Attract sign and allow all the missing soul parts to return from Satan, his demons, their dark storage places, people, places, and heaven, from this time and space and beyond. We can ask them to be cleansed, healed, and integrated where they belong. Then we can ask the angels to clamp the cords to the soul parts twenty or more times, which cannot be brought back at this time, so that Satan and his demons cannot influence people through those soul parts.

Some of my hypnotized patients gave the following descriptions of what happened when I prayed to activate the magnetic sheets:

- "When Dr. Modi asked for magnetic sheets to eject everything that should not be there, they were flying out of there and being collected in the net of Light. I saw nets of Light, which she asked for to collect what is being ejected. I see that they encircle everything, layers and layers of different levels, all going in a circle around everything, and then it breaks down within it around the houses and people and every place it goes. What I see is that the magnetic force is much greater than the suction force and it is more immediate. When the soul parts were being attracted back, it was the electromagnetic transformation. It is like filaments of Light turning from dark to Light. As the soul parts are coming in to where they belong, an imprint of the magnetic energy is put into each being where the soul parts are returned. So it is permanent; it is part of the evolution of life. The magnetic memory stays there and will attract what belongs to it almost automatically. The magnetic recognition is theirs, which is now inside of them. It has now more power than the original one, so that everyone can call back.

    "We need to put the magnetic sheet around the houses and buildings, and everything and everybody in them will be cleansed, too. The energy of magnetism is vertical. It goes up; it does not go down. It will come up from wherever the bottom is. We can leave the magnetic sheet around when not in use. We can put the magnetic sheets everywhere all over the creation, then they can be turned on or off when needed. It is actually very similar to a vacuum cleaner's suction energy. Visualization of magnetic sheets ejecting and attracting with tremendous force is very strong.

"Archangels are saying we also need to ask for the magnetic sheet around an individual home and person because they are all of different qualities that require detailed focus. Timing is like its own little space that will only open up when it is ready. So we can have a magnetic sheet going through, but it will be protected from it because it is not ready.

"Magnetic sheets and triple compression chambers of crystalline Light—once we put them there, people cannot reject them; they stay there. Every time we ask for magnetic sheets to be activated, it happens. It also strengthens everything around. When we ask for expelling and attracting, it does happen, but it does not necessarily affect the free will at a level where danger is perceived. People cannot reject the magnetic sheets, just like they cannot reject sky or the Earth. Magnetic sheets work anyway, whether people are aware of it or not, and changes will happen in time."

ARCHANGEL GABRIEL: Your hand is on the pulse of change of the human evolution and consciousness. Physical evolution goes slower than the consciousness, which is like a great bird that pulls and leads the way to fly higher to God. The magnetic sheet is a way for you to connect with change. When you work with the natural energy to focus your intention and your attention, then you speak your desire. You are working in a multi-dimensional level simply by that particular action. This is assistance for you to move to heaven or any place to qualify what it is you are searching for to bring it to Light. Your job is to bring darkness to Light.

DR. MODI: As I was praying to God and requesting the angels to also put the magnetic sheet around all the sections of heaven, I was thinking of putting the magnetic sheet around everybody in heaven, including people who are in between the incarnations, all the transformed demons we have sent to heaven, because they probably all have missing soul parts somewhere. Is it okay to do that?

ARCHANGEL GABRIEL: Yes! They all need their soul parts back too. You can also ask to put magnetic sheets around the masters and angels you know and do not know because there are multitudes of them. Also, when you ask for masters of astrology, you can ask for masters of less familiar astrology. Every culture, every development, and every human has a relationship to these qualities. You can simply use what God is giving you at each movement to look into, and there would be a reverberation effect.

- "As Dr. Modi prayed for the magnetic sheets to be put around the whole heaven and different sections of heaven, I saw it happening. Magnetic sheets also were being put in and around the section of heaven where all the transformed demons are kept, because they need continuous cleansing and healing and their soul parts need to be returned. Magnetic sheets were also put around all the people in heaven, in between the incarnation and wherever needed, and around the section of heaven where people go for cleansing and healing after the death of their physical body.

    "As the switch of the magnetic sheets around the whole heaven, different sections of heaven, and also around the beings in heaven were turned to the Eject sign, I saw a light grayish cloud of energy coming out of the heaven. It was collected in the net of Light and transformed. When the switch on the magnetic sheets was turned to the Attract sign, I saw soul parts coming back from all over the creation and also from heaven where soul parts of different people were stored. They are going back to humans and other beings going through reincarnations, transformed demons, and also some to the masters and other heavenly beings.

    "You, Dr. Modi, were hesitant to ask for magnetic sheets to be put around heaven and heavenly beings because you did not want to insult anybody, thinking that they might have something negative, but Archangel Gabriel is saying that everyone has something negative, because it is part of creation, it is part of duality, of opposites and the unknown. Your work is impossible to offend. Negativity in heaven is not always in the dark. Negativity is the opposite of the one. One is the Light, and the two is opposite of it. It is Light and negativity in relationship to each other. Sometimes negativity is dark, and sometimes it is the polar opposite.

"The magnetic sheets were put around every section and every soul in heaven, when you asked. It is a continuous process, which is a way of understanding in the dimension of past, present, and future time. It is necessary to be continuous until you and others, you do not know yet, get a greater understanding, because you are bringing this in with your focus and it is happening, but others are getting in their own way."

- "When Dr. Modi asked for magnetic sheets to be put around me, I saw the magnetic sheet almost like saran wrap around me. It is not hard but has a feeling of fluid. I see thousands of dark ones coming out of me when the switch on the magnetic sheet is turned to Eject sign, and they are quite large. I see angels collecting them in the net of Light and transforming them and taking them into the Light. When you asked to turn the switch to the Attract sign and allow all my soul parts back to me, which I lost from the beginning of my existence from Satan, his demons, people, places, darkness, and heaven, from this time and space, and beyond, I saw them coming like a hail or snowstorm. They are cleansed, healed, and integrated with me where they belong."

- "As Dr. Modi requested to put the magnetic sheets around the whole creation, I saw magnetic sheets around the whole creation. Then as you started to break it down to different dimensions and in between the dimensions, around every home, building, structure, street, vortex, water body, and everything else, I saw the energy of the main sheet around the creation spiraling down around everything you asked for. When you went to put the magnetic sheet around the heaven, it was separate. Then when you went to purgatories and the darker places below, that was also separate, but within each separate large sheet there are spirals that go inside everything you described."

- "This time, when you asked for magnetic sheets to be activated, it went into an angle all over. Before, the magnetic sheets were wrapped around a person or a place and were vertical and horizontal, but because it is magnetic, it also went through the body. Magnetic sheets were put everywhere. You did not miss anything, but this time it also went in an angle through everything and everybody, which brings us closer to the higher consciousness. It brings linear and non-linear time closer together, and this will help the self-healing process. Before, I saw self-healing in linear time and it was taking a long time to go through all the generations of healing. This new angular magnetic energy will speed up the self-healing process, because it is going outside of the linear time.

    "The healing is happening for everybody slowly, so their bodies will not explode. Healing has already happened outside of time. The evolution has already happened outside of time, but within time, it has to take its own time and each human, animal, tree, elemental, and dimension has its own progression of evolution. There is a difference between the progression and time. We on earth understand progression of time. We cannot understand it any other way. But there is progression on the other planets and in heaven that is not involved with time; it is involved with concept."

- "When Dr. Modi asked for magnetic sheets to be put around the air and the atmosphere, I saw puffs and clouds of darkness coming out of them and caught in the nets of Light, and the soul parts—the Light comes in and expands the Light, which is there. They almost have emotions and look happy. Before cleansing, there was more of the grayish vortex-like patterns in the atmosphere. The air is the puff that causes it to move around the atmosphere in the space surrounding the air. There are different layers of atmosphere, because when you get outside of the earth's atmosphere, there are layers of other atmospheres overlapping each other."

- "Archangel Gabriel is saying it is important to put the magnetic sheets around the nets, which the first humans brought with them during their first incarnation on Earth. Nets have to do with the perception; it is like a veil over the eyes. My net is the embroidery done by women of nature and art, and the one you have is a sound net, and there is a veil or a net to look through which changes the perception. When you put the magnetic sheet around them, you are clearing them out and making the perception of sound clearer. The demonic energy is the one that changes the perception, so it is the added focus that you are putting on this particular quality of perception and auditory acuity.

  "Archangel Gabriel is saying that you can also ask for cleansing and healing of all the nets that other first humans brought with them. The more you ask, the more it will go in generalized form. For example, when we first gave you the concept of the magnetic sheet, it had a certain visual form, and now it is going deeper showing how it actually works. It is divided into the original power of the request and the forms, which were visualized, which was a sheet, and then it becomes more subtle as you go deeper into the way it works. That makes it possible to go deeper into the form and action that result."

Healing with the Magnetic Sheet

DR. MODI: I request the angels to please put a magnetic sheet all around this person's mind, body, and soul, and also around all the systems, organs, parts, skin, muscles, bones, joints, blood vessels, Kundalini, meridians, etheric nadis, chakra, psychic antennas, physical, emotional, mental, and spiritual bodies, every cell, and all thirty-two strands of DNA and connecting cords to God, masters, heavenly beings, higher self and inner self, and every soul in the creation and heaven.

Then turn the switch in the magnetic sheet to the Eject sign and expel all the foreign entities, dark shields, dark connections, dark devices, dark blocks, dark energies, all the infectious agents, and everything else which does not belong with

73

her. I request the angels to collect everything that is ejected out of her in the net of Light, transform them, and take the energy to heaven.

PATIENT: I see all types of gray and black energies coming out of every part of my body. They are coming straight out. They do not trickle and do not go down at an angle.

DR. MODI: I request the angels to please cleanse, heal, and fill her with the crystalline Light. Please turn the switch of the magnetic sheet to the Attract sign and allow all her missing soul parts to come back to her, which were lost in this life and all the other lifetimes and in between the lifetimes from the beginning of her existence, from Satan, his demons, from people, places, darkness, and also from heaven. Allow them to integrate with her where they belong after cleansing and healing them.

PATIENT: I see an angel turning the switch to the attract sign. Magnetic energy is pulling in my soul parts from all over creation and also from heaven. It is creating an enormous magnetic vortex. It is like I am becoming a vortex for my soul parts. It is the magnetic energy that is making me a vortex. Soul parts of different sizes are coming back to me, and some are very large. For some, it is taking a longer time because they are coming from places which are deep, old, and far away. As they come they automatically get cleansed and healed and are melting within me where they belong. The whole process is very loving and gentle; there is no harshness.

It is almost as if my body is taken over by my soul and is moving through time and the sky layers. The sky also has been there every single time, close to every single body and also has its own layers. My body is moving slowly and collecting my soul parts (surprised). My body is going to different places with the magnetic sheet to find my soul parts, because I have so much of my soul which needs to come back.

ARCHANGEL GABRIEL: She is describing a combination of what has happened in the past, in terms of loss of soul parts. Many of her soul parts have come back. Some of the soul parts appeared very large, because they were connected to the bodies of different lifetimes. Later on, if she wants to know detailed information of some past life, she can get the information from soul parts or the past-life personality of that lifetime. So we can retrieve as many soul parts as we can with high speed to move her energy up, and then we can call small-sized soul parts. That will be the next stage.

DR. MODI: I request the angels to raise the energy level and continue to magnetically attract all her soul parts back, please.

PATIENT: Now I feel that flour-like powder coming back to me, which are very small soul parts. When you asked the energy level to be raised up, my body went to the higher level.

ARCHANGEL GABRIEL: It is a symbol of visualization to take her away from the Earth instead of standing there, grounded with her feet in a lifetime, so she has a larger experience. She is moving out of the body, and we are trying to move her above, because the sky is related to time you will explore later. There is sky that exists now and the sky that existed in the same place 2,000 years ago, but it was another layer of sky in terms of your three-dimensional concept. It is like she is moving out of her body, and now you can call all of her soul parts in through this magnetic attraction from sources all over creation. You do not even have to ask for specific soul parts; ask for all of them to come back to her. They all will be able to come back, as long as you go beyond your immediate concept of time and space.

DR. MODI: I request the magnetic sheet to attract all her soul parts from all over creation, from this time and space and beyond, and allow them to integrate with her after cleansing and healing them and her body.

PATIENT: I see soul parts coming from everywhere and going in every part of my body, mind, and soul. They look like sparkles of different colors, and they are being attracted to where they belong.

DR. MODI: Gabriel, did all her soul parts come back?

ARCHANGEL GABRIEL: Not all. Even though we have gone outside of space and time, she is still in space and time, so there is that duality happening here. Some of this duality you can understand; it has different positive and negative characteristics. She is still on the Earth plane. Her soul parts are coming in, but there are still more. There is a limit to how many soul parts can be integrated at a time; you just accept it for now and ask again tomorrow. You will just know when to use the magnetic sheet again. You have an excellent discernment and knowing. Ask the angels to shut off the magnetic process or turn the switch to neutral and the magnetic sheet will be inactive.

DR. MODI: I request the angels to turn the switch of the magnetic sheet to neutral, to shut off the magnetic process. Cleanse, heal, and fill her mind, body, and soul and every system, part, organ, cell, and DNA, Kundalini, meridians, nadis, and Chakras with the crystalline Light. Shield it with triple compression chamber of crystalline Light, violet shield, mirror shield, and rays of blinding white Light. I pray to God to please fill her with the violet liquid fire and let it blaze into intense flames, non-stop twenty-four hours a day, and cleanse, heal, and realign her DNA.

PATIENT: I see it all happening.

DR. MODI: I thank God and all the beings of Light for allowing her amazing healing. Please continue to cleanse, heal, protect, and inspire us about what else we can do to help. Thank you from the bottom of my heart.

Healing in Heaven

Sometimes patients are able and allowed to see what happens to the souls in heaven and how they are healed.

- "As Dr. Modi prayed, I saw the Light flooding in and bathing everything and everybody in the creation. God put .shields around Satan and his commanders who are bound in space, so they cannot interfere with the session. I saw very dense Light come down through this office and other buildings. I saw that all the souls from the Holocaust, with whom we worked yesterday and sent to Heaven, are ready with their letters to each of the souls they hurt. They are ready to share them simultaneously and ask for forgiveness, so the souls can be healed. They had to do a lot of writing, and the victims are ready to hear them. I am shown that some of the damage that was done to the souls in the Holocaust was so bad that God has to come directly into those healing rooms in Heaven to heal them.

  "I see all people who are under the influence of Satan and his demons (i.e., the perpetrators) revealing not only their life with people of the Holocaust but with all the souls, from the beginning of their existence. They had to go back and clear their karma from the beginning, since the evil began to influence them, and write a letter to each and every soul about what they did to them. I see one of them holding a letter and communicating the information telepathically. The letters are like pages of Light, and the letters are three dimensional. They go to souls who are the victims and clear all the karma. Each person who was a perpetrator in the Holocaust is standing at the top of the line, and there are thousands going back for each perpetrator. A letter is read to each person, and the victims see the letters, hear the words, and get the opportunity to see that the person has transformed, and they forgive him. This goes on for both sides. Those who were victims were also perpetrators in other lifetimes, and they also do the same.

"The Nazi soldier who hurt me is reading me a beautiful letter. He is standing all around me like many selves of himself in many different lifetimes. All the various selves have a letter in their hands, and he is like singing the contents of these letters in the Heavenly sounds. It is more like he is singing me a song as opposed to reading me words, and my soul parts are returning to me with each note. I see all the perpetrators and victims are doing it. The victims stand in the center and see all the lifetimes they had together. The victims get to see all the relationships and all the soul parts coming back to them. It is like this big network of fibers coming out from both of them like a wheel with spokes on it. Here is a victim, and spokes are coming out on each side, and all the souls of the person are in the human form, and they are singing this beautiful music, and each of the souls are healed.

"Then they trade places with each other, and the victim who was a perpetrator sings the letters to the other person, and all soul parts are coming back. There is a louder music overhead like the sound of all of Heaven singing right now, and the world is just vibrating. There a massive healing going on all over the Heaven right now, because all the past lives, all the karmas, and all the wheels are turning at once. All the spinning of the vibrational energy that was counterclockwise is now reversed to clockwise. It is just amazing what is going on. It is beautiful; it is like an orchestra or a symphony, and all these souls are being healed, which increases their Light after getting this healing of all the soul parts, from all the vibrations of our existence. Each soul is becoming brighter and becoming a Master. That is a gift of this healing. These souls, who have completed their karma and healing, appear as Light now. This healing was only for the Holocaust victims."

- "When Dr. Modi, prayed for the healing. for every soul on the earth and the whole creation from the beginning of time due to all the tragedies, natural and man-made disasters, and the negative actions, I am getting chills all over because this prayer is very powerful and is granted by God. I see that lots of Light is flooding into the office and the masters, archangels, and angels are surrounding us and sending us lots of love. They are saying to us, 'Thank you for being part of God. Thank you for asking for this healing. Thank you for making it possible to have influence on the souls and heal them: and bring them back to God.'

"Right now I see they are bringing the whole Atlantis into this room and what they are showing is the whole civilization that had so much potential but instead destroyed itself. It shot itself in the foot by becoming demonically possessed. That is why Atlantis had to slide in the ocean. They are saying that it had to happen. They had so much negativity accumulated that there was a giant earthquake and the Atlantis slid in the ocean. They are saying that the remains of Atlantis will be found pretty soon in the future. All the souls from Atlantis are ascending to Heaven and are allowed to heal the same way Holocaust victims were healed. The souls are put in the triple compression chambers of crystalline, white Light, and they are given a deep infusion of Light.

"I see healing for everything and everybody you requested, such as souls from the mass burial sites, all the graveyards, all the sites of battles, people who died painfully in the hospitals, all addictions, all murders, all abuse, all the events connected with painful death, and all the souls coming out of the grips of Satan and his demons. It seems like the whole heaven is expanding. The heavenly beings are saying not to worry; they will not run out of space. The Light of God is very intense. For some of the healing God needs to come very close and literally touch the souls who are extremely damaged.

"I see that every soul on earth is going through a similar healing process. Even the animals, plants, trees, and stones are also going through the same healing process. They have a special place in heaven. There are special places for different vibrations that have consciousness. They have an animal world, a plant world, a stone world, a fish world, an insect world, a bird world, and worlds for all the other beings. I see a lot of souls going up to heaven for healing, especially the chickens and cows who were mass sacrificed. They are sending up the souls of the executioners of the different animals, birds, fishes, and other souls, who are going through the similar healing process. I see the ocean world and its creatures. There are different sections for bugs, insects, and bacteria in heaven. There is also a section for dinosaurs. Everybody is getting healed, because they all died a traumatic death.

"I also see all the pre-humans, the first humans, and all the humans that are there and all the Godheads in the condensed section of energy. They are all very close to God. The masters are like one person. I see God's Light is blazing even more intensely. It is like the ball of God is expanding with all these healings. As the souls are healing and getting all their soul parts back, which they, had lost from the beginning of their existence. They are growing, and as a result, God as a whole is growing and expanding.

"Now I am seeing this office. The Light is just wrapping around it, over, and under, as I see part of God coming out of the void. I see God as a whole is a beautiful sunflower, and I also see God in this office as blazing white Light. We are also getting healed right now. They are saying that we do not have to do anything, just let the Light transform us. 1 see us standing in the oval Light, and our auras are like bright shimmering orange around us. It is as if we have three layers of Light. God is saying that the orange color represents getting our power back. That is why orange is around God right now, as in-the solar plexus chakra, and .that is to make sure that we have our powers as human beings, When we want to feel powerful, all we need to do is invoke that beautiful shimmering orange Light, golden Light, and white Light around us. The Light is orange with silvery white in it. So it is glittery, soft, transparent, and warm."

Releasing Earthbound and Universe Bound Spirits

When I hear about somebody dying in person or on television, the first thing I do is pray to God and request their angels to help them to heaven, and I have faith that it is done. Although my first book *Remarkable Healings* is filled with case histories about the earthbound spirits and how we can help them to heaven, in this book I am including a case history of releasing earthbound and universe-bound spirits.

During a session, as we were releasing some earthbound spirits from a patient, we decided to release all the earthbound and universe-bound entities from all over creation.

PATIENT: When you asked to help out the possessing human or alien spirits from all over the Earth and creation, I saw lots of them coming out, including spirits of children and all other ages and different races. Many are still crouching and hiding inside.

DR. MODI: All the spirits of people who are hiding inside other people, listen to me. Your physical body is dead. This is your spirit body, and you are living like a prisoner in someone else. Everyone after the death of the physical body needs and deserves to go to heaven. There is no punishment or judgment, no matter what you have done. There is only love and acceptance. So come on out. It is time to go home to heaven and rest and heal. Listen to the angels; they are all there to help you to heaven, so walk out of there.

PATIENT: They all turned their heads when you began to talk to them so nicely. They were listening, and they could feel the love you were talking about. Some of them are standing up and coming out, some of them are crawling out on their hands and knees.

They were all bunched up in a corner with their heads down upon their knees.

DR. MODI: We pray to God to please open everybody's connecting cord to you and flood them with Love and Light.

PATIENT: They all can feel the love of God and are coming out of people's bodies.

DR. MODI: We request the angels to please cleanse and heal everybody in whom these spirits were and fill them with the crystalline Light. Bring all their soul parts back, cleanse them, heal them, fill them with the Light, and integrate them with those to whom they belong.

PATIENT: I see they are all being healed.

DR. MODI: We pray to God and request the angels to please put the magnetic sheets around all these earthbound and universe-bound spirits. If it is all right, turn the switch to the Eject sign and eject everything from them that does not belong with them. Collect them in the net of Light, transform them, and take them to the Light. Please fill everybody with the crystalline Light.

Then turn the switch of the magnetic sheets to the Attract sign and allow all the spirit's soul parts to come back that were lost from the beginning of their existence from Satan, his demons, people, places, darkness, and heaven, from this time and space and beyond. Cleanse them, heal them, fill them with the Light, cut their dark connections, and integrate them with whom they belong. Fill every entity with the crystalline Light. We pray to God to please open their connecting cord to you and fill them with love, Light, and joy, and help them to heaven.

PATIENT: I see the healing is being done for all of them. They are happy that their soul parts came back. I can see them. They are all smiling in heaven.

When you prayed for the earthbound and universe-bound spirits to come out from people's bodies, some of them came, but many were hiding inside different humans, thinking no one could find them. I am seeing many children of different ages hiding, with their knees up and heads down, inside different people in the darkness. Those who are less than two years old are out, because they are closer to the Light, but the older children do not want to come out (crying). They are wondering why they had to die.

I see the same thing happening all over creation. There are different extraterrestrial beings in groups, such as beings that resemble insects and others. They are in groups, because that is how they function. A lot of extraterrestrial beings are born at the same time, so they function in groups.

DR. MODI: All the little children all over creation, who are hiding in someone's body, listen to me. Even though your body died, your soul is still alive, and you do not have to be a prisoner in someone else's body. You can come out and go to heaven. Look up and tell me what you see.

PATIENT: They all see heaven and angels stretching their arms out with love.

DR. MODI: Would you like to go with them?

PATIENT: They all want to go with the angels, but the people they are in are not ready to release them, and the little kids do not want to leave them.

DR. MODI: All the little ones, listen to me. As long as you stay inside of the people, they will be sad, because they are feeling your sadness and fear, too. Once you go to heaven, you will feel better, and the people you are in will feel better, too. So come on out and hold the angels' hands and go with them. All those people holding onto spirits of the kids inside their bodies, listen to me. You are hurting them and yourself, so let them go. I request the angels to please locate each and every child who might be hiding and help them out. Cleanse them, heal them, and fill them with love and Light. Bring all their soul parts back they lost from the beginning of their existence. Cleanse them, heal them, fill them with the Light, and integrate them with those to whom they belong.

All the children who are hiding inside people, listen to me. You all need to go to heaven. There is no punishment or pain, only love. So hold the hands of angels and go with them.

PATIENT: (Crying) I want to cry. I did bad things by aborting my babies. Their souls also came out of me. They are all right now. I see all the children's spirits going to heaven.

DR. MODI: What else is happening?

PATIENT: Some of the groups of extraterrestrial souls went up instantly; the others took longer. They all came out through pores of the skin. I saw spirits from many people going to their section of heaven.

It is funny, now I am seeing multiple, extremely large freight-type elevators made up of Light coming from heaven all over the creation to pick everyone up. They have many floors for people at different levels of consciousness. You cannot even imagine how big they are. They are almost as big as the planet they are on. Billions and trillions of souls are lifted out and taken to heaven. I am understanding that there are certain corners all over creation we have not covered yet. There are repeats of certain archetypal behavior that have different dramatic stories in each culture and each universe. It has to be understood that there is a difference between the emotional context of the story and the mathematical energy quality, because even the formula is limited. It does not complete all the meaning. It is more like an idea—that people will build the civilization around an idea, so it is as if the idea has its own personality.

I see the elevators are packed like in rush hour, except the upper levels, because very few souls of higher consciousness stay earthbound or universe bound. The elevators are in the Light, and they are stepping out in heaven. Then the elevators come down again to bring souls who are still stuck or hiding.

DR. MODI: All the people who are hiding inside people, listen to me please. No matter what you have done, everybody is accepted in heaven. There is no judgment or punishment there, only love.

EARTHBOUND SPIRIT: We did not know that. I am speaking for all the spirits of people here. We are the saints and the priests from different religions, and we always talked about the punishment. We scared people to death, and now we are feeling guilty for what we have done. Our egos were so strong that we thought everything we know and talk about is the truth, and now we are afraid that God will punish us. We never looked for confirmation like you do and would be upset if somebody asked us for the proof. We should have been humble, but we were not, and now we want to whip ourselves. There were some spiritual people who tried to tell us differently, but we would not listen to them.

DR. MODI: All of you look inside yourself and see what made you that way.

EARTHBOUND RELIGIOUS SPIRIT: (Crying) I have been a pope and religious leader in different lifetimes and in different religions. All of us have betrayed people again and again because of our egos and pride and by holding onto our belief system, which we call faith, and if we lose that, we lose our power.

DR. MODI: Tell me, why did you cry when I asked you to look inside yourself?

EARTHBOUND RELIGIOUS SPIRIT: I saw something dark in me, which was confusing me. When I was living in the body, and even now, it is like a black shell covering my Light (crying). It is a demon. I cannot stop crying because of what I have done to people and myself. I could not go to heaven; I had to stay here and punish myself.

DR. MODI: No, you do not have to punish yourself. Everybody is accepted in heaven. There is no judgment or punishment by God or any other heavenly beings, no matter what you have done.

EARTHBOUND RELIGIOUS SPIRIT: What about Satan? Will he be allowed to go to heaven also?

DR. MODI: Yes! He is also a part of God. Whenever the time is right and he is ready to go, he will be allowed to go back to God. We are transforming all the demons and sending them to heaven, and they are welcomed there with love. There is no punishment or judgment. If they can be accepted with love in heaven, why not you? Did you watch me working with demons?

EARTHBOUND RELIGIOUS LEADER: Yes, but from a distance. We were hiding deep down. We are all packing up and are ready to go to heaven now.

DR. MODI: Wait, you do not want to go to heaven with the demons in you. We need to remove dark entities, energies, and dark devices from you first. These demons were the ones who gave you the negative information and also influenced you.

EARTHBOUND RELIGIOUS LEADER: I can see the chastisement in the Catholic religion by whipping yourself until you bleed is put in by the demons. Oh, God, I can see so many things in the Bible that are inserted by Satan, such as "God will punish you and send you to hell," "We only live one life," and "Jesus is the only son of God." I can see it is not true, because we are all children of God. These are all inserted by Satan into our belief system.

DR. MODI: Do you realize that when you whip yourself you are losing multitudes of your soul parts, which are grabbed and held by Satan and his demons, and then, life after life, they have control over you through those soul parts.

EARTHBOUND RELIGIOUS LEADER: (Crying) Oh, God, I can see how we damaged ourselves life after life, and how Satan has inserted things through people who were writing or translating the Bible and other religious scriptures.

DR. MODI: Yes, all the religious scriptures are gifts from God, but Satan and his demons have also managed to insert wrong information. You can think of it as contamination by the dark side. So when you read the scriptures and something does not feel right, pray and ask for the truth and guidance, or tune into your soul and ask for the guidance. Do not follow everything blindly, but discern what is true and what is not.

EARTHBOUND RELIGIOUS LEADER: How about people who suffer terribly on Earth? Is it not a punishment by God?

Dr. Modi: No! God never punishes or judges anyone. People, with the help of Satan, are choosing to go through that suffering. God gives us free will to choose whatever we want. He and heavenly beings will never interfere with our free will unless we ask for help, but Satan does not care to honor the free will of people. He intrudes and interferes with us and our lives.

Earthbound Religious Leader: Who created the fire in hell?

Dr. Modi: Satan! He created it to torture souls who are taken there, to scare them, so they will follow him and his demons' instructions faithfully.

Earthbound Religious Leader: We feel that you are giving more therapy to us than spirits of lower people who went to heaven first (embarrassed). Here is our arrogance again. We think of ourselves as upper class and all the other people as lower class who went before to heaven.

Dr. Modi: You know that is not true. You people have your fixed beliefs, which were difficult to change, while other people did not have that problem, so they went to heaven faster.

Earthbound Religious Leader: Now we are ready to go.

Dr. Modi: Not yet. We have to remove those demons from all of you and do the healing, and then you can go. How many of you are here?

Earthbound Religious Leader: Multitudes of us are here from the beginning of time and are not able to go back, and many are lost through different time periods. Some of us are here because we misused sexuality and preached that sex is evil. Some of the Catholic priests here abused boys sexually. I feel we did not go to heaven because we have to have this conversation and understanding.

Dr. Modi: We pray to God and request the angels to please collect in the net of Light and remove all the foreign entities, dark shields, dark connections, dark devices, and dark energies from all these earthbound spirits. Transform them, cut their dark connections, and take them to heaven. Cleanse them, heal them, and fill them with the crystalline Light. Then bring all their soul parts back that they lost in this life and all their past lives, from the beginning of their existence, from Satan and his demons, from people, places, darkness, and heaven, from this time and space and beyond. Cleanse, heal, and fill them with the Light and integrate them with whom they belong. Clamp the cords to the soul parts that cannot be brought back at this time.

PATIENT: The demons coming out of these religious earthbound spirits are very thin, and there are big Lights in them, which come out and get bigger and bigger. These are the soul parts of these religious leaders.

DR. MODI: One of the demons can speak for all the other demons collectively. Tell me, how did you affect these religious leaders?

DEMON: We essentially affected individuality, creativity, and sex. Out of that came pride and false humility, and out of that came others. These are very sensitive souls, and we come in when they are infants and young children. By the time they are five, we have taken control of them. We continue to influence them all their lives. We are the ones who infused the idea of celibacy in Catholic priests; it is an unnatural requirement. It is the idea of sex being evil, and if you give in to sex, you are out of control and will create confusion in society. The flow of their creative energies is also impeded. We create a robotic behavior in them and make them scream as they are preaching, which turns people off from listening to them.

DR. MODI: I request the angels to please locate every soul part of people who were traumatized and fragmented while listening to religious leaders in churches, temples, or other religious places. Bring them back from Satan and his demons, from people, places, and darkness, from this time and space and beyond. Cleanse them, heal them, fill them with the crystalline Light, and integrate them with those to whom they belong after cleansing and healing those people.

PATIENT: I see it all happening.

DR. MODI: Dark ones, one of you can speak for everybody. The Light is around you for a while. How does it feel and what did Satan tell you about the Light?

DEMON: We were told to stay away from the Light, because it will burn or destroy us, but it is not (upset). He lied to us.

DR. MODI: Yes! Now look deep within your being, your core, and tell me, what do you see?

DEMON: (Surprised) A tiny spark, and as I am looking at it, it is growing, and I am all Light in no time.

DR. MODI: Do you feel dead?

DEMON: No, I feel better and more alive and bigger. Can we help Satan to change into Light?

DR. MODI: We are helping him little by little, and he is about to change, but still it will take a long time for him. We have bound him and his big commanders into space and have emptied, cleansed, and healed the dimension that used to be hell.

DEMON: Yes, but when the preacher preached about hell, it became activated again, so we kept some of the fire in hell going.

DR. MODI: We pray to God to please send the tornado Light through the dimension that used to be hell and suction out everything that is dark and negative. Transform them and take them to heaven, please. Bring all the soul parts back that belong to the dimension of hell, cleanse, heal, and integrate them where they belong. Cleanse, heal, and flood that place with the crystalline Light and shield it with the triple compression chamber of crystalline Light, violet shield, mirror shields, and rays of blinding white Light. Fill it with the violet flame and let it blaze nonstop as long as it exists.

MUSLIM EARTHBOUND RELIGIOUS LEADER: We mullahs [religious leaders] think of having exclusivity of God; we think only our Allah exists. We want you to work with terrorists and help them because they are listening to those mullahs, also Chinese religious leaders who are also preaching against sex and other things. Please work with them; they also need help.

DR. MODI: We pray to God and request the angels to please lift all the dark and other entities out of all Muslim, Hindu, Chinese, Christian, Jewish, and all the other religious leaders all over Earth and creation. Cleanse them, heal them, fill them with Light and love, and shield them with the triple compression chamber of crystalline Light, violet shield, mirror shields, and rays of blinding white Light. Remove all the soul parts of different people, cut their dark connections with Satan and his demons, and integrate them with those to whom they belong after thoroughly cleansing and healing them. Help all the demons to transform into the Light and help them into the Light.

MUSLIM EARTHBOUND RELIGIOUS SPIRIT: We are mullahs joining with Chinese leaders who are not religious leaders, but we are working hard to stop the religion in that country. We mullahs did it by focusing on power. Anyone who felt powerless, we focused into blame and exclusivity of our God, who is a vengeful God and will punish those who caused us suffering. They believed everything we told them, because they do not have much freedom in our culture. They are suppressed, and we reinforced the desire for revenge because we feel we are the only true religion. The Catholics believe the same way, that their religion is the only religion.

There are devices, like bellows, inside and outside of people. We encourage people to get angry. There is porousness inside the consciousness of people that matches what surrounds them. We keep people in small groups, so they can match others in their small groups. In America, people have come from other parts of the world. They are forced continuously to deal with other groups. We lie that physical death is rewarded in heaven.

DR. MODI: To the Chinese leaders, one of you can speak. How did you affect people in your country?

EARTHBOUND CHINESE LEADER: Well, we had a lot of help from the government. Their great lie was oneness of all. For generations, they made everybody wear blue clothes. We became more and more regimented by speaking of freedom. The more we spoke of freedom, the less there was. There was a lot of intelligence. We ripped out all the religions, because the government said all religion is evil. Here, politics is our religion. We do not want humans to connect with nature, because they will feel the Light of God, so we put them in prisons. We are communists—the religion of the state.

DR. MODI: We pray to God and request the angels to please remove all the foreign entities, dark shields, dark connections, dark devices, and dark energies—transform them and take them to heaven, please. Then bring back all the soul parts of all these earthbound spirits who were lost in this life and all the other lives, from the beginning of their existence, from Satan and his demons, from people, places, darkness, and from heaven, from this time and space and beyond. Cleanse, heal, and integrate them with those to whom they belong.

PATIENT: I see it all happening.

DR. MODI: All the transformed demons, do you choose to go to the Light?

TRANSFORMED DEMONS: Yes, please.

DR. MODI: You have done a lot of damage to all these religious leaders and people they preached to. What do you want to say to them?

TRANSFORMED DEMONS: We are sorry for what we did to you. Please forgive us.

DR. MODI: Are they all forgiving you?

TRANSFORMED DEMONS: Yes!

DR. MODI: Do you all choose to go to the Light?

TRANSFORMED BEINGS: Yes, please!

DR. MODI: All of you, we send you home to the Light with love. Go in peace. Goodbye.

TRANSFORMED BEINGS: Thank you.

EARTHBOUND SPIRITS OF RELIGIOUS LEADERS: Before we were standing, and now we are sitting down. We are just shocked as we watch all these demons changing into the Light. So we are sitting down for a while. The Light expands rapidly in the darkness. We are very grateful for this experience. We ask all the humans and beings of the whole creation for forgiveness for what we did to them through our ignorance, and they are all forgiving us. We were feeling guilty about it, and now it is gone and we feel better, but we still have a hole in our heart and need healing for it.

DR. MODI: We pray to God and request the angels to please bring all the soul parts back that were lost in all lifetimes and also from the beginning of their existence, from Satan and his demons, from people, places, darkness, and from heaven, from this time and space, and beyond. Cleanse, heal, and integrate them with those to whom they belonged. Fill them with the crystalline Light and shield them with the triple compression chamber of crystalline Light, violet shield, mirror shield, and rays of blinding white Light. Heal and expand their heart and soul. All of you, how do you feel?

EARTHBOUND SPIRIT OF RELIGIOUS LEADERS: The hole in our heart is healed, and Light has expanded tremendously.

DR. MODI: All of you, do you choose to go to the Light?

EARTHBOUND SPIRIT OF RELIGIOUS LEADERS: We beg to go to the Light.

DR. MODI: All of you, look up and tell me what you see?

EARTHBOUND SPIRIT OF RELIGIOUS LEADERS: The Light is enveloping us and welcoming us. There is no judgment, criticism, embarrassment, or shame. Just love.

DR. MODI: All of you, we send you home to the Light with love. Go in peace and go into the Light only. Good-bye. I request the angels to escort them to the Light, please.

Earthbound Spirit of Religious Leaders: Why don't you come with us? We do not want you to die. We want you to come to the Light and have a tea party with us. We are happy for what you did for us.

Dr. Modi: Maybe I will come in the night. Right now, you need to rest and heal.

Earthbound Spirit of Religious Leaders: Okay. Thank you!

Dr. Modi: Bye! We request the angels to please thoroughly cleanse and heal all the churches, temples, mosques, and all the places of worship, and the vortexes under them and miles and miles around them. Flood them with the crystalline Light and shield them with the triple compression chamber of crystalline Light, violet shield, mirror shields, and rays of blinding, white Light. Create the centers of Light around them and let it extend into every room and every section of those places. Thank you.

Patient: I saw a lot of darkness coming out of those places, including from the benches and other furniture, so when people sit on them, they get engulfed by the darkness.

Dr. Modi: We thank God and all the beings of the Light for helping us in releasing all the earthbound and universe-bound spirits. Please continue to cleanse, heal, protect, and guide us in the right direction. Thank you from the bottom of our hearts.

People in a Coma

People under hypnosis often describe that people in comas have a major portion of their soul outside the body and a smaller portion is still stuck inside. Sometimes they see a spirit or a soul part of their children or other family member holding on to the soul and do not want it to leave them. Other times there are demons that are holding on to their soul for different reasons. As a result, the soul is unable to come out of the body completely. It is in between life and death; it cannot live and function fully because part of the soul is outside and cannot leave because a portion of the soul is still stuck in the body.

A friend's ninety-two-year-old mother was sick for a long time and was in a coma for a while. During one session, we decided to work and heal her and all the people in a coma to whatever extent was allowed by God.

DR. MODI: We pray to God and request the angels to help each and every person in comas all over the Earth and creation. Please help everybody's soul to come out if part of it is stuck in the body and cannot come out. Also, those souls that are confused and not quite sure whether they want to live or die, help them make a decision and help their souls to go in to the body completely or come out of the body and go the heaven. Please free every soul who is in a coma.

PATIENT: It is almost like I see one person who represents all the people in a coma lying in bed. He has a very dark face. It is the dark energy covering his face. I see part of the person's soul is out and a larger portion is still stuck in the body. It seems frozen and waiting. I see an ugly-looking demon overlapping the soul and not allowing it to move.

DR. MODI: We pray to God and request the angels to please collect in the net of Light all the demons, dark energies, and spirits and soul parts of other people from this person and all the people who are in a coma and lift them out. Cut their dark connections and fill every person who is in a coma with the crystalline, white Light.

Separate all the demons, human spirits, and energies. Cut their dark connections with Satan, his demons, and the people they were in and transform the dark entities and energies into the Light and take them to heaven, please.

PATIENT: I saw the dark demons and energy being transformed and taken to the Light. Then it's funny, I saw a big shovel made of crystalline Light, like a scoop that lifted out whatever was left over. They were transformed into the Light and taken up to heaven. There are different things happening with different people. Some people are moving into the Light, some people are waking up a little bit and feeling alive. Their souls completely moved back into the body.

I am seeing your friend's mother. Part of her is floating above her body and part of her soul is inside. She is not sure what she wants to do. It feels like she has to decide whether she wants to leave the body or go back in and live some more. More of her is inside then outside. I think you need to help her.

DR. MODI: Aunty, please listen to me. Part of your spirit is outside and part of it is still stuck inside. You are suffering a lot, and you do not have to. If you choose to leave the body, you can, but if you choose to still live, you can. We can help you to come out of the body or go back in. Since your body is sick and not functioning well, if you feel it is time to leave the body, you can. You do not have to suffer anymore. If you look up, you can see all the masters you believe in and the angels are all there to help and welcome you.

PATIENT: It is so beautiful I want to cry. She heard you and sees the masters and angels in the Light. They are stretching their arms out, and she is gently coming out of her body. There are many angels wearing outfits of different colors helping her.

She is saying that she is going to go back in and say good-bye to all her family members and then she is going to leave. She is out of the body but staying close to keep it warm.

DR. MODI: What was the problem why you could not leave?

MOTHER: People did not want me to leave them. They wanted my presence, my love and comfort, and I was torn between what to do. They felt safe in my presence. Now I will leave after seeing them one more time. Thank you for your help.

PATIENT: She is putting her arms around you and giving you a kiss. It seems like part of your soul went where she is. She seems very peaceful. All the other people in a coma all over the earth and creation also heard you and were able to leave their bodies. There are some who are still unable to leave.

DR. MODI: We pray to God and request the angels to cleanse and heal all the soul parts that came out from all the people in a coma. Cleanse them, heal them, and integrate them with whom they belong.

PATIENT: I am almost seeing like a policeman directing the traffic. There is a lot of traffic here. Some soul parts are going to heaven and others are going to different people and integrating where they belong after completely being cleansed and healed. The people in a coma who did not go to heaven are completely in the body and are resting peacefully.

DR. MODI: We pray to God and request the angels to cleanse and heal everybody who is still in a coma and fill them with the crystalline white Light. Bring all their soul parts back that they lost from the beginning of their existence. Cleanse them, heal them, fill them with the Light, and integrate them with whom they belong. Then whenever they are ready, help them to heaven please. If they need to heal, please heal them.

PATIENT: Around the third week or so in January I see some of them sitting up, while others are resting peacefully.

Three days later, my friend's mother died peacefully, after she said goodbye to everybody in her large family.

Satan and His Demons

Working with spirit release therapy and releasing human, alien, demon, and other spirits under hypnosis for about twenty-five years, I have realized that Satan and his demons are the main source of our physical, emotional, mental, spiritual, and relationship problems. They are also the main reason for our personal, family, and societal discords and also the cause of conflicts between two or more people, groups, countries, or religions, leading to arguments, fights, and wars. They pull the cords to our soul parts, which they have in their possession, and we act like a puppet in their hands. Most of the time we are not even aware of being manipulated by them. In *Remarkable Healings* I have given a lot of information about Satan and his demons in detail along with many case histories. Heavenly beings have always suggested that we should pray regularly for cleansing, healing, and removing all the human, demon, and other spirits and all the dark devices and dark energy, filling everybody with crystalline white Light and shielding us with the triple compression chamber of crystalline Light.

Also in the future there will be a book about the story of Satan: his creation, building his empire, how he influences beings all over creation, the transformation of hell, and binding Satan and his top commanders in the space and his future. Following are some examples of how they work and affect us.

- "When Dr. Modi prayed for the connecting cords of every soul and dimension to God to be opened up and be allowed to feel the connections and become consciously aware that there is something beyond themselves, I saw it happening to every soul. I also saw the cords to demons opening and the beams of Light going to them, and they were kind of becoming shocked. They were turning round and round, looking like a black ball, doing somersaults. They looked like they were having convulsions. They were trying to curve their bodies around themselves into a round ball, so they would not have to feel the Light. As I look at Satan, he is bound in his cage of Light in the space, and the cage shrinks and becomes tighter around him. He is lying on his back and trying to push the cage of Light away from him. He looks thinner since we took out multitudes of the soul parts of people and places out of him. He is shaking and turning side to side. He is leaning against and hiding something like a rock. He has pointed wings like a bat and is wrapping his wings around it, but I can see it underneath. It looks like the tub of the volcano.

"When Dr. Modi prayed to God and requested the angels to put the magnetic sheet around Satan and all of his demon commanders who are bound in cages in space and all the other demons, and all their storage places, turn the switch to the Eject sign and expel everything from them, whatever is allowed at this time, I saw a rock came out from under Satan's wings, and they collapsed. The rock was like a geometric design of the pyramid but upside down. Now he is sitting up straight, and from every cell of his body, something came out. I see multitudes of soul parts of Earth and all the living beings on Earth and all over the creation are coming out. I am seeing many soul parts of demons are also coming out of Satan.

"I see that soul parts of creation are all tangled. They look like they are hanging on a charm bracelet. What I get is that these are the archetypes of forms. These are the original souls of the whole creation. What is so amazing is that out of the top of his feet, between the heel and the toes, a lot of feet soul parts are coming out. I have a vision of all the bound feet of Chinese women. I am seeing these women's feet, of each layer of time in history of all beings that had ever had a lifetime there who are alive now. Their feet are exploding now like a beautiful lotus flower. Feet are flying open now, and those flowers are blooming in everyone's feet. Now Satan's feet look flat, and everything in his body is skinny.

"When you asked everything negative to be ejected, which came in because of the small shoes being put on, I saw everything negative coming out of people's feet, collected in the net of Light, transformed, and taken to the Light. I also saw terrible shoes for women that have been designed throughout the history where heels are very high and the pointed narrow toes, the memory and reminder of the small feet. This is due to the demonic influence in people who design these types of shoes to create the similar terrible discomfort. At the same time, the creative Light part in humans is creating the running shoes."

- "Satan was never obese, but there is a relationship between Satan and the obese people. The energy inside Satan between his bone structure and the outer epidermis has layers inside. It is all puffed out, as if it were the pages of a book. So the cover of the book is like the epidermis, which is hard. His whole body is being compressed. He has tremendous magnetic force inside of him. That is why magnetic sheets went close to him. The space between Satan's bones and epidermis was like air; it was the negative fat he had. The fat in humans has something that holds in the dark energy as negative fat. I see millions of soul parts coming out of different people as negative fat. Some of them are still left in him.

  "Satan and his demons take the soul parts from fat people, which are like puffed-up air. I see that Satan and his demons pinch and pull on people's soul parts, and as a result, they want to eat more because they feel uncomfortable and unhappy; they eat for comfort. The demons also use devices to inject the air in people, which causes discomfort. Here the body of Satan is like a warehouse, which has collapsed now, so the cover of the book is on the top of the pages, and there is no air or soul parts in between. The humans may still feel some discomfort and anxiety but much less. Everything is removed from Satan, transformed, and taken to heaven.

  "When you asked all the negative fat and air to come out, I could see yellow fat turning to liquid. People might get diarrhea, stomach cramps, and aches and pains all over the body. I also saw all the last thoughts, decisions, promises and all physical, emotional, mental, and spiritual problems are being released on your request from different lifetimes from the beginning of our existence which are responsible for our weight problems.

"I see all the soul parts are coming back like a Lightning bolt from Satan, his demons, from people, places, darkness, and heaven, from this time and space and beyond. They are integrating where they belong. Then everybody was cleansed and healed with the crystalline Light and then the violet flame. Now Satan looks like a skeleton. His whole body was layered as a dictionary of recipes and formulas for destruction. Now there is no fat, air, or spaces left in him.

"Archangel Michael is saying to pray for the Light in Satan and his demons to be expanded. Pretty soon they will complete this part of their mission and will have another job. Satan is slowly remembering about himself and his future. He knows a big change will come for him.

"When you prayed for Light of Satan and his demons to be expanded, I could see the Light within them becoming larger."

One of my patients saw a soul part of Satan inside of her. Following is a transcript:

DR. MODI: I request the angels to collect this soul part of Satan in a triple compression chamber of crystalline Light, lift it out of this person, and bring it outside her shield. Satan, tell me why you are here in her?

SOUL PART OF SATAN: (Angry) I do not want to speak to you.

DR. MODI: Tell me, how did you affect this person?

SOUL PART OF SATAN: I was sleeping a lot, but I had more power in sleep. I told her she was the devil, and her nanny also told her, because she could sense I was there. Even the nanny had a big part of me. I gave her fears, making her feel like she was evil, and she had a constant preoccupation with it. I took away all the good feelings she had about herself. Anytime she was complimented about anything good, I made her feel it was a lie. It was endless, and she was never sure about herself. I had to be sleeping somewhat to slow her down.

DR. MODI: I request the angels to transform this soul part of Satan into the Light and take it to the heaven.

PATIENT: He seems to have the memory of weeping. It feels like he wants to weep. He has not wept for eons of time.

DR. MODI: Michael, is it time to get the information from him about Satan and his history?

ARCHANGEL MICHAEL: With the compassion, sadness, and tenderness in this soul part of Satan, it might be possible to get the information from him.

PATIENT: Wow! I can see Archangel Michael. First I saw him as the common image, then I saw him as white, very large and covered by sparkles of Light. He has all ages in him; he is young and strong, and he is also wise and old. He has all the potential. I feel there is a lot of interference coming from Satan in space, so we cannot communicate with this soul part of Satan at this time.

DR. MODI: Michael, can we put a shield around the cage of Satan, so he cannot interfere with this soul part of him?

PATIENT: He put a golden shield around the cage of Satan that looks like golden mercury, thicker than honey with the white in it. He is completely covered with it. This way, Satan will be less able to interfere with his soul part whose memories can be activated, so there can be a worldwide satanic shakeup. Michael is saying that he can freeze Satan's soul part in time while you work with other things, and then you can work with him. I see Satan's soul part in a frozen block.

Florescent Lights

One of my patients had migraine headaches off and on for a long time. Under hypnosis, she found many layers of demons and dark devices and traumas in multiple past lives that were responsible for her headaches. She also described fluorescent light as one of the sources of her headaches as follows:

PATIENT: I am seeing that fluorescent lights also trigger migraine headaches in me. What I understand now is that they have lower vibrations. Heavenly beings are telling me that the fluorescent light is also influenced by Satan and his demons. It creates mood disorders by sending out black rays, which make a subtle sound and have negative vibrations. It gives a color of light that destroys the natural spectrum of Light. Heavenly beings are saying that we should restrict the use of fluorescent light as much as possible because it has black rays, which influences other colors of light negatively, and that is the reason why other colors do not seem right in fluorescent light. Even the ones which are used in homes for money saving, long lasting light bulbs, are really not good. The reason they are not as harmful is because they put a coating of yellow color on them to give them a warm and natural color. As a result, the glass that they shine through makes the black rays less harmful. Fluorescent light puts people in a bad mood and makes them agitated and restless. It interferes with learning and concentration. If in the schools, the lights are changed from fluorescent to candescent, there can be a noticeable improvement in ability levels.

I am shown that Satan has a special factory where he creates black rays to be infused into the fluorescent lights. I see only one factory. It is like a gas factory. As the fluorescent tubes and bulbs are made on our planet, there are demonic devices coating all the fluorescent lights with black rays. It is actually the fluorescent light, which is mixed with the black gas and put in fluorescent tubes.

Now I am shown Satan's factory, which looks like a black bubble or a black cylinder where the demons are mixing up the black gas inside. Then in the factory on earth, the tanks in which humans put the gas to put into fluorescent tubes, the demons put the black gas in the form of black bubbles, which dissolve in the tank of the fluorescent gas, and then they are put into fluorescent bulbs and tubes.

So the black gas bubble is made in Satan's factory. Then it is sent through a dark tube inside the tank that holds the fluorescent gas where the black bubbles dissolve and release the black ray paper gas. Then the gas is dispensed to fill the fluorescent tubes.

When you, Dr. Modi, prayed to God and requested the angels to dissolve and transform Satan's factory and the black gas and take the energy to Heaven, I see the angels putting the triple compression chamber of Light around the factory and lifting it up to heaven along with the demons and the black gas. The demons are very confused and upset and do not know where they are being taken, and Satan cannot do a thing but watch it happen helplessly. In Heaven, the Light is concentrated in the chamber and dissolving the black bubbles, and the demons are changing into Light. They are also taking the soul parts of people out of the chamber and transforming them and healing them.

DR. MODI: We also pray to God and request the angels to please lift out all the dark gas bubbles from the factory on the earth and from all the fluorescent tubes and bulbs, and from people wherever they may be, take them to Heaven in the triple compression chamber of Light and transform them. Then cleanse, heal, and shield all the fluorescent tubes, the black bubbles or rays, including the people.

PATIENT: I see it all being done. Heavenly beings are still suggesting to get rid of the fluorescent light, because it is not the pure spectrum of Light. It is a bad invention and was inspired by Satan. Today's healing will improve the vibrations, but it will still be advisable to replace it with regular light bulbs, because it blocks the Light and guidance from heaven. The area where the factory was, is cleansed and healed, and all the missing soul parts are brought back which belong to that area and integrated after cleaning and healing and shielded with the crystal shield, metallic shield, and mirror shield.

Bug Repellent Device for the Insects

- "When you prayed for the removal of insects from your home, Archangel Gabriel is saying that bug repellent devices for the insects are harmful to bugs and also to humans. Use them briefly and do not overdo it. You should not keep it plugged in all the time. It interferes with the level of sensitivity and perception, and it creates a blocking effect. You can put in the instructions that it will not affect you. Insects are telepathic, so you can also ask them to go elsewhere. You need to speak to their leader that you prefer they leave; it is not appropriate for them to come into the house. You need to thank them for coming to make you aware of their presence and tell them that they are part of God and do not need to make humans aware of their presence by annoying them. Take the plugs out for a few hours and tell them not to come back. You could also ask that the sound from these devices not affect you in a detrimental way. It creates fear and discomfort. It is like someone screaming at you. It is very dark and negative. It is based on fear instead of compromise. You need to compromise with them, because they are trying to get your attention by annoying you. Talk to them and their leader."

Viruses

- "When Dr. Modi prayed for the H1N1 and all the other viruses and infectious agents to be suctioned out, transformed, and taken to heaven, I saw it happening all over the Earth and creation. It came out like breath from all the people, hospitals, places, air, from people in groups such as subways, schools, and places where people come together, stations and offices where there are not many windows and air conditioners. I saw it happening all over, except in some places. Sometimes it is necessary for some lessons. My higher self is saying that viruses are beings that are influenced by demonic energies. When the immune system is compromised, consciousness of all the people needs to be lit. They need to become aware of themselves and of their own purpose. Demonic influence in the virus makes people susceptible. We should pray regularly to increase our immune system to the highest normal limit."

Haunted Houses

- "When you prayed to put the magnetic sheet around all the haunted houses and turn the switch to the Eject sign, I saw lots of black demons coming out wearing different types of black costumes."

Fear

- "As I look at the whole creation, it is the single misty gray cloud that represents the fear. It is enormous, about a billion feet high. It was symbolic of everything that came out of creation. It had different shapes and images in different dimensions, different planets, and different aspects of creation."

Patient's Hump in the Back

- "I saw enormous pieces of Satan that are related to the Earth coming out of my hump in the back. There are about twenty of them, and they have a cord that is pulling into the Earth. I see that we all have a connecting cord to mother Earth. I see that my hump in the back is collapsed now."

Healing of Divas and Elementals and Their Dimensions around the Earth

During one session, my higher self-suggested that it is important to work with elementals and divas. They bring the Light on the planet Earth and thus help in maintaining the balance. There is not so much darkness in them, but it is the environment that they are in that makes it harder for them to be happy. They are not so happy when they get tired. It is as if they are surrounded by the mud and cannot move quickly. The darkness in the atmosphere around the elementals makes them uncomfortable. They are doing their work anyway, but they are not so happy. What makes them happy is to spread their Light everywhere, just the little sparks of Light. They are heavenly.

Diva energy is similar to fairies and nature spirits. Divas are nature spirits who are holding the pattern for the nature spirits with whom they belong. They are the creation of God. They are like an oversoul to the souls of the nature spirit.

According to heavenly beings, there are following main elementals on Earth:

Earth Elements—Gnomes, Kobolds, Giants

Water Elements—Undines, Nymphs, Nixies, Naiads

Air Element—Sylphs

Fire Element—Salamanders

Gnomes

One of my patients recalled a past life when she was a gnome, which will be described in detail in the next publication. Following is a portion of that past life.

- "When you prayed to God to cleanse and heal all the gnomes who were living in that life, I saw white shimmering Light, like diamonds, filling and healing us. All the soul parts were brought back and integrated, and everybody was healed. My past-life personality as a gnome was cleansed, healed, and integrated with me.

  "I am seeing a huge dimension parallel to Earth for the gnomes, and it was fairly dark before you cleansed and healed it. Most of the parallel worlds, parallel to Earth were influenced by the demons, and now they are all cleansed, healed, and shielded at your request.

  "Archangel Gabriel is saying that many of these parallel worlds were dark and getting cleansed and healed every time you continue to ask for their cleansing and healing. Once they are not so differentiated then they are integrated. There is not much darkness now in these parallel worlds, since you have been clearing and healing them, but memory of the dark time is still there. Once the darkness is also cleared from memory, then they do not remember those things and the past is rewritten. The past gets changed, and the dark memories do not exist anymore. The same is true with human beings and all the other souls.

  "It is like when you were working with the large soul part of Satan and when you transformed him into the Light, he remembered his name as Lucifer and did not want to remember what he did as Satan. He said you have to ask the part that is still Satan, and he will tell you. When these parallel dimensions are cleared and there is no darkness anymore to feed, the dimensions will collapse. There is a parallel to everything: a parallel universe, a parallel world, or a parallel thought."

Mermaids

One of my patients recalled a past life when she was a mermaid, which will be described in detail in a future publication. Following is a portion of that past life.

• "On Dr. Modi's request, all the missing soul parts are brought back for the mermaids and humans, including to me and you, Dr. Modi. The dimension of mermaids and all other dimensions around the Earth are cleansed and healed, and all the missing soul parts are brought back and integrated where they belong after cleansing and healing. Then all the dimensions and all the mermaids, mermen, and humans were shielded with triple compression chambers of crystalline Light, violet shield, mirror shields, and rays of blinding white Light. All their connecting cords to God were cleansed, healed, and opened up. I saw their connecting cords to God becoming clear and larger.

Fairies and the Middle Earth

One person during a session saw a connecting cord going from me to a fairy princess in another dimension. The following is the transcript:

PATIENT: I see a beautiful fairy princess lying down. She looks very tired and drained.

DR. MODI: Fairy Princess, you have a part of my soul. How did you get it?

FAIRY PRINCESS: We are soul mates. We were one soul at the beginning, and then we were split into two separate souls and are living different existences.

PATIENT: She is lying down because she is feeling very tired due to a great deal of demonic influence in their dimension called the middle earth. This fairy princess and other beings of middle earth are very empathetic, and that is why they could not stay on earth. They feel the pain of everyone: earth, animals, trees, and humans. I see a great deal of darkness all over the middle earth and everybody on it.

DR. MODI: I request the angels to please collect in the net of Light, all the dark and other spirits, dark shields, dark devices, and dark energies from all the middle earth people and the whole dimension of the middle earth. Lift them out, help them to the Light, or bind them in space. Remove and transform what needs to be transformed and take the energy to the Light. Scrub and scour, take away any residue that is left over and fill the space with the Light. Bring all the soul parts to the middle earth and its beings that they lost in this life and all the other lives from the beginning of time, from Satan, his demons, from people, places, and darkness. Cleanse and heal them, fill them with the Light, and integrate them with whom they belong. Clamp the cords to the soul parts that cannot be brought back at this time. Fill them with the Light and shield them with triple net of Light, violet shield, metallic shield, mirror shields, and rays of blinding white Light.

PATIENT: I see all different types of beings of middle earth in a circle, and there is fire in the middle. There are sparks coming out of the fire, which are the soul parts and going back to whom they belong. The sparks are also going in their third eye.

DR. MODI: Please flood the whole earth and the middle earth and all their beings with the violet liquid fire and let it blaze into violet flames. Fairy Princess, tell me how do you feel.

FAIRY PRINCESS: Less tired. We may need more healing later on sometime.

PATIENT: I see white Light flooding into middle earth and its beings, pushing out all the dark entities and energies out of them, which are lifted out by the angels and taken to heaven. Then the angels brought all their soul parts back and integrated them where they belong. I see their connecting cords are being opened up and violet Light is flooding in and transforming the whole middle earth and their beings.

I see the fairy princess and all the beings looking more energetic and smiling. There was a dark shadow all over the middle earth and all its beings. It was draining their energy and causing dread, which they felt, and we were experiencing it too, to some extent. Now it looks like sunshine, and there is more peace and harmony. I see a dark soul came and took their will and hope away, leaving them in deep despair, depression, and fatigue.

DR. MODI: We pray to God and request the angels to please bring all the soul parts to hope and the will power of all the beings of middle earth and integrate with them after cleansing and healing and flood the whole middle earth and its beings with love, joy, hope, healing, and energy. Cleanse and heal all the parallel universes throughout creation. Shield them completely with triple compression chamber of crystalline shield, mirror shields, and rays of white Light. Open their connecting cords to God and guide them in the right direction. We pray to God to please flood the whole creation and everything and everybody in it with the violet liquid fire and let it blaze into intense flames. Transform and realign their DNA and heal them please. Thank you.

PATIENT: I see it happening all over the creation.

DR. MODI: Fairy Princess, what else can we do to heal the middle earth and its beings?

FAIRY PRINCESS: I do not know yet. Right now we feel like we are waking up from sleep. But check back with us again.

Parallel Dimensions around the Earth

According to heavenly beings, there are about twelve bands of Light or dimensions around the Earth. They are all part of heaven and are outside of time and space. There is a dimension for elementals, and each elemental has a section in it where they retire. Insects have their own section, while trees and plants have a different level of heaven because they stay. They do not die. Their consciousness moves into the other tree. If there are no trees left from a certain species, that pattern of that tree will go to a part of heaven that is like an Akashic record of the history of the trees, and it is also like a storehouse of consciousness. The trees are considered a life form. There are areas, or levels, that are the level of masters of the species. Everyone has a master above them in heaven. They are a part of the Alohim group to keep on creating the life form. They incarnate from time to time to see what they have created. There is a separate dimension for fairies with hills, trees, and flowers that other dimensions do not. They are etheric beings who appear to clairvoyant people.

- "I see about twelve parallel worlds around the planet Earth, which are overlapping each other. They look like dimensions around the Earth. They are of different qualities, depending on what is inside each one. Some are overlapping, some are not. The fairy dimension is a little bit different in shape and has trees, hills, flowers, and nature scenes. Others with a small lifespan have a narrow band of just Light, and there is just the consciousness of the souls, which have computer-like feelings. All these dimensions, or bands, are outside of time, so they can operate with more fluidity. They are all etheric. Life forms go inside these bands or dimensions around the Earth. I see the band of insects next to earth then there is a big band around for the elementals, which is divided into different sections for different elementals."

- "When Dr. Modi prayed to cleanse and heal all the etheric dimensions and places around the earth, and all over creation that are partially in the world of Light and partially in the world of form, I saw the magnetic sheets around them sending the magnetic energy through etheric dimensions and curving around each dimension. It loops down and around, sending the magnetic energy all the way through. Then when she asked for negative energy to be ejected, I saw all these black arrows coming out. They are going out in every direction and are caught up in the nets of Light by the angels. Then when the magnetic sheet switch is turned to the Attract sign, I see soul parts coming from everywhere. I see people and beings all lined up to receive their soul parts. It is like an announcement was made. All the different types of elemental beings also were cleansed and healed and got their soul parts back. Then on Dr. Modi's request, all the dimensions around the earth and all over creation and all their beings were shielded with triple compression chambers of crystalline Light, mirror shields, and rays of blinding white Light. They also created the centers of Light around those dimensions throughout the creation."

Healing of Planets of Our Solar System and Their Masters

During a session, archangels suggested that I speak to different astrological masters of our solar system and do the healing of our solar system and their masters. All these masters are connected with all the humans and are involved with different aspects of our life. Most of the information will be given in the future publication. Following is the healing information.

Master of Neptune

One of my patients had a big soul part of Satan in her that was trapping many soul parts of the patient and master of Neptune.

DR. MODI: I request the angels to cleanse and heal these soul parts of this patient and Neptune. Fill them with the crystalline Light and integrate them with this patient and soul part of Neptune to Master Neptune in heaven.

MASTER NEPTUNE: Thank you. I am grateful that you integrated this part of me. There are many more of my soul parts out there that need to be integrated with me.

DR. MODI: I request the angels to bring each and every soul part of Master Neptune from Satan, his demons, people, places and darkness; cleanse them, heal them, fill them with love and Light, and integrate them with him, please.

PATIENT: The first thing I saw was multitudes of Neptune's soul parts coming out of Satan, who is literally lying on his back with his stomach open because he had devoured these soul parts. They are also coming from other planets. Then I saw lines and lines of psychics and wise men, shamans, alchemists, medicine men through history that used Neptune's energy. They were sitting there with their costumes. Many psychics were using the energy because of satanic influences. It was the level of consciousness shared by all psychics and wise people outside of time and space, because Neptune represents the levels of consciousness. All the soul parts of Neptune were cleansed, healed, and integrated with him. Now he is looking better, more muscular.

DR. MODI: Neptune, did you get all your soul parts back?

MASTER NEPTUNE: (Happy) I am happy to have so many of my soul parts back. Maybe you should check again.

DR. MODI: We pray to God to please send the Lightning bolts to all the soul parts of Neptune throughout creation, wherever they may be!

PATIENT: I see multitudes of his soul parts coming from all over creation: from Satan, his demons, people, places, and the darkness, and integrated with Neptune after cleansing and healing. He looks very happy to get all his soul parts back.

ARCHANGEL MICHAEL: Neptune is an ancient icon, an ancient symbol of seas. In the ancient times, it was the God of the sea when the planet of Neptune was discovered. The qualities that psychics and astrologers noticed came at a time when there was no difference between good and evil. The boundaries were very misty. It represented the magical and spiritual energy and all possibility without judgment.

The most important part to remember right now is that Neptune does not know the difference between right and wrong; that created problems for humans. It is mysterious and mystical. It is the energy of the spiritual communion. All astrologers and psychics use that energy to make predictions and give advice to their clients. Some of them do not know that it is Neptune energy. The essential energy represented by Neptune has been flawed because of its murky boundaries. It moves to a level where good and evil are not important. It is more important to sense the continuity without a definition, so there is a positive aspect to this energy. True understanding of the difference between good and evil has been removed, and this soul part of Satan has that energy in him and played an important role in this person's life. It cut short any good feeling about what she has done and experienced. It caused her to doubt and think that anything good she has done has an underlying evil element. The dark parts and energies need to be cleansed, healed, and transformed into the Light. They have a long history from the beginning of the creation of all life and planets.

DR. MODI: Michael, is there a demon commander for each planet of our solar system?

ARCHANGEL MICHAEL: Yes, but you can work with all of them together and with the top commander, which is Satan himself because the spiritual aspects bridges specifically between heaven and Earth. Every human and living being has an aspect of Neptunian energy. This is why it is very important for Satan to use that energy to manipulate human beings, especially when there is confusion between good and evil. This is where Satan can persuade people that something that is evil is very good. There is a separate demon commander for each planet, and one top demon commander for all the planets, because there are different requirements, mythologies, and abilities, and a different sense of good and evil. But there is always a limitation in all planets where there is a difference in the balance of various energies.

PATIENT: Neptune looks happy, bigger, and strong, and says he wants more of his soul parts back. He looks like the picture of the Greek god Neptune.

DR. MODI: We pray to God to please send lightning bolts to all the soul parts of Neptune, wherever they may be in creation; transform and allow them to come back and integrate with Master Neptune and his planet, wherever they belong.

PATIENT: I see the Lightning bolts are going to many sealed cabinets which are opened all over the creation. Soul parts of Neptune are coming out and going where they belong on the Neptune planet and to Master Neptune. Lightning bolts were like keys to the cabinets. It seems Neptune is standing here, and all the soul parts of planet from all over creation are coming to Neptune. His energy is very adaptable.

ARCHANGEL MICHAEL: What makes it so attractive to Satan is that after they were in people, the Neptunian energy muddled the truth and caused confusion. The true energy of Neptune is that all things are possible. There is confusion because the discrimination of continuity of ideas has been removed. If not used properly, Neptunian energy can be dangerous, because there are no boundaries.

DR. MODI: Neptune, did all the soul parts come back to you?

MASTER NEPTUNE: Not yet.

ARCHANGEL MICHAEL: Neptune is represented with the ocean and fishes; he is the king of the sea. So you must ask the soul parts to come back from all humans, all the water bodies, and their creatures, and even the fluid in the human body.

DR. MODI: Can we put on the magnetic sheets?

ARCHANGEL MICHAEL: Yes; put it around all the water bodies and everything that is liquid, lives in liquid, is surrounded by liquid, human bodies, which have liquid, trees, which have sap in them, flowers with liquid in them, the whole creation, and every planet that has liquid in some form.

DR. MODI: We pray to God and request the angels to please put the magnetic sheets around all the water bodies and all the creatures, plant lives, and everything that has water in them.

PATIENT: I see magnetic sheets going around the Earth and all the planets throughout creation, around all the water bodies and all the creatures and plants in them, and the entire plant kingdom. I see angels lined up for further instruction.

DR. MODI: I request the angels to turn the knob of all the magnetic sheets to the Eject sign, and expel all the dark entities, energies, dark devices, dark shields, dark blocks, soul parts and spirits of other beings, and collect them in the net of Light. Transform them into the Light and take them to heaven, please. Cleanse, heal, and fill everything with the crystalline Light.

Then turn the knob of the magnetic sheet to the Attract sign and allow all the soul parts to return that were lost from the beginning of time from Satan, his demons, water bodies, and life forms in them, people, elementals, creatures of all types, plant life, places, darkness, and heaven from this time and beyond. Integrate them where they belong after cleansing and healing.

PATIENT: I see all this happening, so fast that it is hard to describe.

Master of Mercury

DR. MODI: We pray to God and request the angels to put the magnetic sheet around the planets Mercury and Earth and all the other planets connected with them, including the DNA strands. Can I put the magnetic sheet around the masters and other beings of heaven too?

MASTER OF MERCURY: Try and see what happens. This is powerful; it works with time and is very fast. The magnetic sheet has a powerful force of expulsion to it. It is like an atomic bomb, but more powerful. So try putting it around all the masters and heavenly beings and see what happens.

DR. MODI: We pray to God and request the angels to please put the magnetic sheet around Master of Mercury, all the masters of Light, and all the beings in heaven, including the people in between the incarnation and transformed demons, and all the areas of Akashic records. Turn the switch to the Eject sign and eject everything that does not belong there. Collect them in the net of Light, transform them, and store them in heaven. Flood them with the crystalline liquid Light; cleansing, heal-

118

ing, and removing everything left over. Then turn the switch to the Attract sign and allow each and every soul part to come back that they lost from the beginning of time—from Satan, his demons, from people, places, darkness, and from heaven, from this time and space and beyond. Cleanse them, heal them, fill them with the Light, and integrate them with whom they belong or where they belong. Clamp the cords to the soul parts that cannot be brought back at this time, twenty or more times as needed.

PATIENT: I see things are being ejected from everywhere and collected in the nets of Light; they are transformed and taken to heaven. I see the nets of Light are put in the void all around the planets and dimensions. They stretch out and become larger as more things are ejected. Soul parts are coming back from everywhere, and they spin as they come out. Darkness comes out, and the soul parts are instantly cleansed and healed, and they become crystalline and get integrated where they belong.

DR. MODI: We are connected to higher self, heavenly guides and angels; and all humans have darkness. So can the darkness go to them from the humans?

HIGHER SELF: Yes! They can come through the connection but instantly change into the Light. They cannot stay dark. Sometimes you also need to cleanse the Akashic records.

DR. MODI: Mercury, did everything get cleansed and healed?

MASTER OF MERCURY: Yes. The mind is observing and receiving instructions and deciding what to do next. Any part where natural progression is being interfered with, needs to be cleansed and healed. There is a big change as you cleansed everything. It is as if a thousand million eyes are opened up; it is like we all sort of woke up and blinked our eyes. The change in you will be that you will find your keys—your missing keys. When you find them, doors will be opened.

PATIENT: I see that the DNA strands are more translucent.

DR. MODI: We pray to God to please fill the whole creation and heaven and everything and everybody in them with the violet liquid fire and let it blaze into intense flames, non-stop twenty-four hours a day, as long as our soul exists. Please, transform and realign our DNA's.

PATIENT: It looks like gas burners lighting up with the purple flame all over creation. The violet flame is more refined in heaven.

Master of the Sun

MASTER OF SUN: The healing of Kundalini was very helpful; I did get a lot of soul parts back. I did not pay attention to it before, but now I am becoming aware of them. I am living in a very extended timeframe, and I see things from a very large perspective, unless it is necessary to focus on a detail. When humanity invented those astrological signs, I could see what they were doing, and that was interesting. I can see how they are affected, but I am more concerned with the critical mass, as the people on Earth talk about.

DR. MODI: What will happen to you after the transition of Earth to the fifth dimension?

MASTER OF SUN: Nothing much because the transition is in consciousness. The transition that will affect many elements that I impact on Earth and all the planets will relate to each other, because of the particular configuration at that time, and it would be a great opportunity for multiple leaps. I am constant, and changes do not affect me.

It is a wave of understanding, and when more of my Light is understood, the astrological signs will change. They will expand. There will be cellular changes in humanity over a period of time based on changes in consciousness and the instructions to their bodies. The bodies are there to accommodate the conscious energy of Light and beings. It is a cooperation between the limited physical perceptions, which evolve in a limited way, and expended souls of external consciousness.

Unless you point it out, I just accept whatever comes. I am the most accepting of the energies and maintain the stability of the Earth and of all living things in this solar system. I am like a big brute here. I am a big, strong element, and it is necessary to filter my energies. Every human, plant, and animal has the mechanism built in to filter me, including the original design that I do not shine on the entire planet at the same time, so there is a cooling-off period. Then the planet is rotating, but I am fixed and do not move. The planet rotates on its own axis around me, so there is enough variation. All the planets have different rates of rotation. I do not get excited easily. I am very calm.

Master of Saturn

DR. MODI: Master of Saturn, yesterday we worked with the demon commander of "Change" and did a lot of healing. Did you and all the planetary masters and planets in our solar system get healed too?

MASTER OF SATURN: Yes, lots of soul parts were brought back. Planets are a whole different story. There is darkness in evolution and there are beings, which are consciousnesses that live on all the planets. These consciousnesses are multi-leveled, so they can be considered beings. It is very hard to describe. We all are affected by everyone, so the healing you did yesterday involved almost a Saturnion—a return to Saturn as proper function—because proper function is what we insist on. We are like the guardians. A lot of darkness came out, and soul parts were brought back. There is a lot of Light in the planet now. It happened for all of us and the planets. The energy expanded and it makes us happy. There can always be more happiness, more joy, more understanding, and more creativity.

It is like discovering more consciousness of God. The human spirit can bi-locate as a being of Light, since their body is still alive and can join with our energy, evolving the whole humanity in unimaginable ways and evolving the structure of the body. We have some understanding of all the possibilities until they happen within time, because we are all working in various aspects of time. All individuals have their own time around them and are a center of their own universe. It is hard for people to imagine that (laughing). It is nice to laugh. I, Saturn, do not laugh too often.

Master of the Moon

DR. MODI: Are there any negative effects of the Moon?

MASTER OF MOON: There are no negative effects of the Moon, except the demonic interference. All those stories of vampires, werewolves, and people acting crazy during a full moon are because I affect people's emotions. They feel their emotions with more intensity, and if there is a great demonic interference, they become out of control, but my energy is loving.

DR. MODI: Is there any other way you affected the Earth?

MASTER OF MOON: These are the basic effects then you can go into effects on individuals. That is why astrology is helpful because individuals can go deeper, as you go deeper with your patients through therapy. Astrologers see what the influences were at birth and how they worked because there is an imprint at birth of a particular set of relationships with the planets. There are also genetic imprints, so there are many complex influences.

DR. MODI: Is there a demon commander who is assigned by Satan to interfere with the moon?

MASTER OF MOON: Yes, there is a demon commander, along with multitudes of demons under him, who are responsible to influence and interfere with the energies of the moon. A lot of the demonic influences were already cleared up as you worked and transformed different commanders. It helped a lot, and there is more Light and hope on Earth now. You will not see it right away, but more and more people are becoming aware of the changes. When you work with the Master of Time then other layers of demons will be removed.

Master of Planet Pluto

DR. MODI: Do you have a lot of dark influence?

MASTER OF PLUTO: My energies are affected the way I affect people. That is where the dark influence is, and I could use some of my soul parts back. We all can get our soul parts back, because as people misuse our energies or stop short, the demonic interference comes in and we feel frustrated. We are just here without being able to do much.

DR. MODI: That is what we are going to do when we work with the demon commander for the Sun of our solar system. We will get the soul parts back for all the planets, their beings, and the ruling masters.

MASTER OF PLUTO: That will be good.

Master of Taurus

MASTER OF TAURUS: Astrological signs have an image; they have a planet from where they get energy, like I get from planet Venus, which also gives energy to other signs. The magnetic sheet is a way for you to connect with change. Your job is to bring the darkness to the Light. You can also ask to put the magnetic sheet around every master, because we all have missing soul parts, too. There are multitudes of masters you do not know yet.

DR. MODI: Thank you for the information. I pray to God and request the angels to please put the magnetic sheet around Taurus, Tobias, and all the masters and beings in heaven. Turn the switch to the Eject sign and expel everything that does not belong with them. Collect them in the net of Light; transform them into the Light and store them in the heaven. Flood them with the crystalline, liquid Light and remove whatever is left over. Then turn the switch to the Attract sign and allow every soul part to come back from Satan, his demons, people, places, darkness, and from heaven, from this time and space

Shakuntala Modi, M.D.

and beyond. Cleanse, heal, and integrate them with whom they belong.

PATIENT: I see only a little bit of gray energy coming out and multitudes of soul parts coming back for Taurus, Tobias, and other masters and heavenly beings. They are integrated with whom they belonged after cleansing and healing.

MASTER OF TAURUS: Thank you! Many soul parts came back to me. I feel better now.

Healing of Alien Races

Sometimes patients under hypnosis recall being abducted by alien beings at different ages. They give detailed information about their abduction, such as who abducted them, why they were abducted, how they were abducted, where they were taken, what was done to them, how they were brought back, and how the experience affected them. Over the years, we have helped and healed many alien races and their planets who were under the influence of demons.

Many times during a session, aliens try to interfere from their spaceships by using the laser beams and causing drowsiness in patients, or create problems with tape recorders or other electronic equipment. Sometimes brand new batteries will go dead. These tape recorders or batteries would begin to work after the session or if taken to the other room. Most of these aliens were under the influence of demons and were possessed by them and were totally under their control. Most of this information will be described in detail in a future publication.

Aliens Causing Sleepiness During a Session

During a session with a patient, all of a sudden my eyes began to close irresistibly. I was feeling sleepy and my eyes were closing and I did not have much control over it. So I asked my hypnotized patient to look around and check if anything or anybody was trying to influence me. The patient saw about six aliens in a smaller spaceship about twelve feet in diameter. These aliens look like humans but shorter, about 4 ½ feet to 5 feet tall. They seemed to be very shy. They put a clamp type of devices on both of my upper eyelids, making my eyes close. So I requested the angels to remove the devices from my eyelids, transform them and take the energy to heaven and cleanse, heal and fill my eyelids with the Light. I requested the angels to bring my missing soul parts to my eyelids back from Satan, his demons and from people and places, and integrate them with me. After removing the clamps and healing my eyelids, I did not have the problem.

During the next session the same thing happened again and the patient saw the same alien beings in the spaceship trying to observe what we are doing. They also put the same clamp type of device on my upper lids, causing my eyelids to close. So I requested angels to remove those clamps and bring all my soul parts to my upper eyelids and integrate them with me after cleansing and healing my eyelids and the soul parts and it was done. Then I requested the angels to bring these alien beings in the office so we can communicate with them. They brought human like aliens who were about 4 ½ to 5 feet tall and were very shy. I asked them why they were interfering with us. The conversation went as follows:

ALIEN BEINGS: We are observing people on many different planets to see what they are doing and learn from them. We are observing you because we want to learn about spiritualty. People on our planet are not spiritual at all. We want to learn about spirituality from you. We have your soul parts from the life when you were living on our planet in a past life. These soul parts were attached to the clamps and this way we could connect with you. We are trying to get your attention by making you sleepy with the clamps. You have planned to help us in this life.

DR. MODI: Tell me, do you know of God?

ALIEN BEING: We have heard about Him but do not know much. We want to learn about Him and how to become spiritual.

DR. MODI: Can everybody on your planet hear me?

ALIEN BEING: Yes, they can.

DR. MODI: All of you please pay attention. We pray to God to please open everybody's connecting cord to You and fill everybody with love and Light. Everybody look up and tell me what do you see?

ALIEN BEING: (Overwhelmed) We all can see God at the other end of our connecting cord and we can feel the love and Light streaming to us from Him. We have never felt like this before. Thank you.

DR. MODI: All you have to do is pray and ask and it will be provided. Every one of you has a piece of God within which has all the knowledge and you can tap into any knowledge you need. So pray and meditate and you will be given what you need. We pray to God to please bless all the beings on that planet with whatever they need. Please speak to every one of them and tell them whatever they need to know. Listen and tell me what He is saying.

ALIEN BEING: He is speaking to everybody on our planet. He is saying, "You have everything you need within you and you do not have to look anywhere else. Just pray and ask for what you need and you will be provided. Just stay in touch with me and ask and be in peace."

DR. MODI: We pray to God and request the angels to please put the magnetic sheets around their planet and everything and everybody in it, including their dwellings and all their transportation vehicles including all their spaceships. Turn the switch of the magnetic sheets to the 'eject' sign and eject everything dark and negative from their planet and everything and everybody in it. Transform them and take them to heaven. Then turn the switch on the magnetic sheets to the 'attract' sign and allow each and every soul part to come back to the planet and everything and everybody in it. Cleanse, heal and integrate them with whom or where they belong. Clamp the cords to the soul parts that cannot be brought back at this time. Fill the whole planet and everything and everybody in it with the crystalline white Light and then with the violet liquid fire. Shield them with the triple compression chamber of crystalline Light, mirror shield and violet shield. I request everybody's higher self, guides and angels to stay on guard around them and protect and guide them in the right direction.

PATIENT: I see it all happening.

DR. MODI: Alien beings, remember; now you do not have to watch and learn from anybody. You have everything that you need within you. You also have God, your higher self, heavenly guides and angels who are with you all the time. So pray and ask for guidance.

ALIEN BEING: We all thank you for your help.

DR. MODI: You are welcome. We thank God and all the Light beings for the healing of these alien beings and their planet.

Alien Interference with the Tape Recorders

During a session, the tape recorders stopped functioning due to interference from alien beings. After we worked with the issues and cleansed and healed the whole alien race and their planet, the tape recorders still did not work. So I asked Archangel Gabriel for the reason, and he gave the following information.

ARCHANGEL GABRIEL: These aliens are trying to get close, like that other group of innocent aliens who were in the school, the first group that you worked with. These aliens are attracted, and they are not aware or do not care about their interference. They are like someone in the line who is desperate to push forward. They do not understand the love the way you do. You need to make them understand about love by working with them. They are trying to get something you have and are doing everything possible to get it. So you need to find a way to give it to them, so they can leave you alone. They are not going to stop until they get it. They want love, Light, and their own incarnations in their own forms. There are layers of groups; when you change the attitude of one group, they will all change. There is a commander within the level of aliens. There are different alien groups that have different amounts of Light, which changes.

There are some alien beings that do not have the top commander. Only the very dark aliens have a demon commander who influences them, and there is a top demon commander for all the aliens.

Demons Working with Alien Spirits

During a session, a patient saw a large demon stretching all over her spine. It was uncooperative, angry and growling.

DR. MODI: Dark one how old was this person when you joined her?

DEMON: (Growling and clenching his fist) You have no power here. I am very powerful.

DR. MODI: I request the angels to surround this demon in the net of Light. Squeeze it tighter and tighter. Shake lose all this person's soul parts and free them please.

PATIENT: This demon looks like a grasshopper type of alien.

DR. MODI: Dark one, what are you? An alien or a demon?

DEMON: (Screaming and growling) I am taking over her.

DR. MODI: Screaming does not mean power. All soul parts of this person come out of that dark one. You do not have to be trapped in the darkness. So walk, walk, walk until you see the Light. I request the angels to help all the soul parts of this person to come out of this demon. Cleanse, heal, and fill them with love and Light, cut their dark connections with Satan and his other demons, and integrate them with the patient please. Lift this dark one out of her in the net of Light.

DR. MODI: What were you told about the Light?

DEMON: The Light will fry me up and kill me. What is it around me? It is not the Light, because I am not frying. So what is it?

DR. MODI: It is the Light. Satan lied to you. Light does not fry or kill. There is another lie he told you. Look deep beneath the layers of your darkness, within the core of yourself, what do you see?

DEMON: I see this alien being, which is still in me, that looks like a grasshopper.

DR. MODI: I request the angels to bring that alien being out of this demon. Cleanse and heal him. Cut his dark connections with this demon and other demons, Satan, his dark centers, or spaceships. So dark one, look deep beneath the layers of your darkness, within the core of yourself and tell me what you see.

DEMON: (Irritable) All right I will look. I see a little flicker of a white thing. It is growing and swirling, and my darkness is disappearing (anxious). It is chopping me. I am almost changed except for my neck!

DR. MODI: I request the angels to cut all its dark connections with Satan, his spy commanders and other demons, dark centers, aliens, or their spaceships.

DEMON: (Relieved) Now I am all Light, and it feels good. I have wings.

DR. MODI: Now tell me, how did you affect this person?

TRANSFORMED BEING: I had that grasshopper type of alien being. I was chosen by Satan to have a spirit of an alien being. There were several of us. We worked with the alien spirits. These aliens worked with her before. So we got in the same way they did. I made her feel like she was taken over.

DR. MODI: Transformed being, move back in time before you became dark, before you went with Satan, recall who you were and where you were.

TRANSFORMED BEING: (Surprised) I am in the Light with God. I was flying to another planet to transport Light energy to create plants, foliage, and leaves. The angel who is here to help me was also working with me. We are taking energy from one planet to another planet. One day I heard a voice. "We want help here." So I looked over there, and I got pulled into him, and it swallowed me up like a snake. It took me down to this big pit. It was heavy and gray there. I could not move. He told us we have to work for them. There were four commanders there. They took us all out of the pit and took us to another room. They taught us about planets, traveling, and spaceships. They told us how spaceships work. We used alien spirits and their ships to interfere with people of earth and other planets.

Alien spirits had soul parts of people, which gave us more power. We could take alien forms by having their soul parts in us. I could enter through the soul parts of different people who were abducted by these aliens. We abducted this person three former lifetimes. This lifetime we abducted her seven times at ages of three, seven, twelve, sixteen, seventeen, twenty-three, and thirty-two years of age. We took more of her eggs, which gave us more power.

DR. MODI: I request the angels to locate all the soul parts of this person and all the other people that are on the spaceships with aliens and demons. Cleanse, heal, fill them with the Light, and integrate them with whom they belong. Clamp the cords to the soul parts that cannot be brought back at this time. Help all the alien spirits and demon spirits to heaven and totally destroy all the spaceships.

PATIENT: I see all this happening.

DR. MODI: Transformed Being, do you choose to go to the Light?

TRANSFORMED BEING: Yes! Please!

DR. MODI: I request the angels to help this being to the Light please. Transformed Being, we send you home to the Light with love. Go in peace.

PATIENT: I see angels bringing all the soul parts of me and other people on earth from Satan, his demons, aliens and their spaceships and from people, places, and darkness. They are integrating them after cleansing and healing, with me and other people. They took all the demons and alien spirits to heaven and destroyed their spaceships and transformed the energy and took it to the Light.

I see an alien device in front of my sexual chakra going through the funnel to the back of the chakra, which interacts with the base of the spinal cord. It is diverting the energy, which is meant to go through the kundalini, down to the reproductive area, and Light was directed out of the body through masturbation and unloving sex, instead of being used to power the kundalini and the chakras. They are organic type of devices, which feed on the Light as well, and they get bigger and healthier. When I did not masturbate over the years, I was able to keep the Light and the devices shriveled up, and they became non-active.

When the devices were originally inserted by the aliens who were used by the demons during the masturbation or through unloving sex, there is loss of a lot of Light—the life force (the soul parts) and demons grabbed hold of the soul parts and used them to manipulate me. It is like the Light bleeds out of the body and inhibits the spiritual development of the individuals.

Healing of Spiritual Channels

Kundalini, Meridians, Nadis, and Chakras

When I prayed for cleansing and healing of the Kundalini, my patients under hypnosis gave the following information about what they saw.

- "When Dr. Modi prayed for cleansing and healing of kundalini, there was a greater flexibility in the channel that it travels through, therefore more power can go through. The healing of kundalini will change anxiety, insecurity, and false self-importance. People will be much more truthful of themselves, because that is the only way to get to the next step of problem solving. The problem solving at every level will be better, clearer, and more exciting. There will be more happiness and joy after discovering a solution without having to stay away to get rid of the interference.

  "I see the kundalini, starting from God and then going to the center of the whole creation, and then it is breaking down to individual globes and dimensions and then to individual beings. It is a fractal concept of repeating the designs. Kundalini is like an umbilical cord to God. I see kundalini going to every being in heaven also. It is exactly the same design, which repeats in everything. A message when it goes through one, everyone throughout the creation gets it, depending on the intent."

- "From the other end, I see kundalini energy as a life force that goes upwards in a straight line through the center of a body, through a planet, a solar system, galaxy, universe, and the whole creation, whatever it is, and then to God. Kundalini is the action of the greater force of Light going through a tube.

I also see kundalini as a caduceus with a center part around which the snake-like forms twist. Everyone has a kundalini.

"Meridians, nadis, and chakras all emerge from the kundalini and are part of the kundalini. They are like the breakdown of the kundalini. They are points within the kundalini. Kundalini is like a tree with branches, which are meridians, nadis, and chakras. The tree penetrates the original DNA in the circle, waiting to be programmed into wherever it needs to go. There is a different concept, so you can experience them separately. When you activate the kundalini all the chakras, meridians, and nadis are also activated because they are part of it. The flow of kundalini energy goes through every chakra. If there is a blocked chakra, it has to do with the consciousness. I see chakras as vortexes; there is a parallel within everything. It is like one energetic form of life, and then it appears in every form. Even the inter-dimensional spaces have consciousness. So wherever the life and consciousness exists, there are kundalini and chakras."

- "I saw kundalini of the whole creation as a long line that goes from the bottom to the top. It is like a straight line that goes up and down throughout the creation. It goes up to the middle of the spiral. The Kundalini is the central vortex in a sense, a central pole that holds everything structurally. It is a passage for the energy of life."

- "What I see is that the whole creation and every dimension and soul has Kundalini, chakras, meridians, nadis, grids, DNA, and different bodies. There is the same replica for everything in the whole creation. That is the fractal concept. Then it breaks down as it gets into more detail. The quality of the energy that flows through the DNA of each life form is a set of instructions for that particular life form. Even within the DNA, there is a flow of kundalini and meridians, because it is the road through which the energy travels giving the instructions. It is the application within the instruction.

"I see that the Nadis are placed differently. They have a different relationship with kundalini than the meridians. They are different points or centers of energetic operation. From each point or center, it stretches out what is equivalent to veins and branches. Again, it is like the seed of the concept, the seed of the idea, seed of the instructions, the seed of the wish, and the seed of desire, and then it stretches out energy that has every quality of attraction and repulsion. It has two qualities related to every possible new concept, like an automobile would have a stop and start, going forward and backward, so these would be the opposites, the equivalent to attract and reject on a much smaller level. These are like pressure points. The point is where it starts and then the energy moves through and it connects to other sections, such as to the chakras and different parts.

"Everything comes from the kundalini. It is the central distribution of energy throughout the entire system, so when the focus is on the awakening of kundalini, all the energy is charged with a greater focus through that one center. When the action is requested or meditated or focused upon, then the energy brightens. The focus of any attention or intention is almost the same thing. Within time, there is a difference, a very subtle difference.

"I see that Chinese meridian pressure points and pressure points for nadis are separate points to focus on. They are separate systems. Chinese pressure points could activate both meridians and nadis. They are like "Y" plugs that can be plugged into two separate recorders. They are two separate systems that can be connected. The entire human body can be seen as one hollow container of Light. Such an intention visualized and desired is strong enough to activate all the system."

• "I see kundalini as a vertical energy in the spine. Then as you kept on adding kundalini of planet, solar system, galaxy, universe, and of the whole creation, I saw all going off vertically at angles. It was traveling like a snake throughout the creation.

135

I see that the whole heaven was also covered by the kundalini, and they are all vertical. They look like caduceus. When Dr. Modi prayed for magnetic sheets around the kundalini, I saw lots of darkness expelled out of all the Kundalini all over the creation, collected in the net of Light, transformed, and taken to heaven. Then as you asked all soul parts of all the kundalini to be attracted back, they were coming from all around rather than from one direction, from different places all over the creation."

- "The device interfered with my sexual function and funneling of the Light around the sexual chakra. It funneled the Light away from the base chakra and interfered with its spiritual growth and rise of the kundalini energy. The device also gave me the desire to masturbate. I lost a lot of soul parts through that. It also blocked my natural sexual expressions in a free and loving way. They enforced the feelings of shame and guilt around the active sex. As the Light in kundalini rises, it empowers each chakra as it goes through them. The chakras are like a flower and signifies the rising of spiritual awareness. If this kundalini energy is funneled out or blocked from rising up the spine, it blocks the spiritual development."

Healing of Medulla Oblongata

According to heavenly beings, the medulla oblongata is the spiritual nerve center of the human brain. It represents the higher function of the spiritual body. It is a spiritual generator. There is a lot of Light in medulla oblongata. When it is blocked by the demon beings, people do not get the spiritual energy to sustain the functioning of their psychic antennas and psychic senses, such as clairvoyance, clairaudience, clairsentience, etc. The person's connecting cord comes from God, goes through the crown chakra, and all the Light communication is interpreted in medulla oblongata in a way that the brain can understand. The demons try to block medulla oblongata, which connects with the human senses. By targeting it, they cut a persons' communication with God and keep them in the dark. Cleansing and healing of medulla oblongata, the spiritual nerve center, is very important for everybody. You should also put on the helmet of Light for protection after cleansing and healing.

- "On Dr. Modi's request, everybody's brain, medulla oblongata, spinal cord, nerves, and the whole body is cleansed, healed, and shielded throughout the creation, and the shield of a Light helmet is put over everybody's head and neck. The helmet is made up of Light of rainbow colors providing different energy to different areas. Now people will be able to get the spiritual information, messages, and divine inspiration and understand them properly."

Healing of the Halo

One of my patients had traumas to her head in many past lives damaging her halo. She gave the following understanding about it.

- "I see that Satan and his demons tore and damaged my halo in many lifetimes. After recalling these traumas from those lifetimes and bringing all the soul parts back that I lost during those traumatic events, we were able to heal my halo. The halo looks like part of the silver connecting cord to God where it enters the aura, crown chakra, and the head. It has layers of Light like the layers in the aura. It has the energy of different intensities and has a higher concentration of Light. I see the halo as being horizontal as well as vertical and it has a lot of depth to it. It expands and grows as we evolve. It also has to do with psychic senses of seeing, hearing, and feeling and is like a protective shield around them. It is supposed to filter what you receive. I see this halo as channels of Light that are connected to and distribute the Light of God to the whole spiritual being, such as all different bodies, aura, chakras, meridians, kundalini, and the soul. Everybody has a halo that can be seen by psychics. When people grow spiritually, the vibrations of their halo also increase. More spiritually evolved people have a more pronounced halo."

Christ

During a session when I prayed for the understanding of the word Christ, Archangel Gabriel gave the following information.

- "When Dr. Modi prayed for the understanding of the word Christ, Archangel Gabriel explained that Christ is the brotherhood of man as one, recognizing itself as the reflection and child of God in every human. It is called enlightenment in some religions, which means the closer understanding and widening the channel to God. It is receiving all instructions and messages absolutely coming from the mind of God. The soul in every person is a piece of God, which becomes Christ when it becomes enlightened.

  "Jesus was an advanced human who gave the message that people in certain numbers were ready to hear. Jesus and his disciples were simple people. It was cutting out the brutal hierarchy into the brotherhood and equality of love in men. It was his main message. It was the priests with demonic influence who made Jesus the only son of God, so they could be intermediaries. It was the demonic interference that created separation of the individual connection with God.

  "Archangel Gabriel is saying that in the Christian religion, Jesus is the only Christ they recognize. But the fact is that there are many beings that have attained the Christhood in all religions, and every human being is a potential Christ, the level available to everyone, which they can activate in time. Christ level is what the Christians call the son of God, and it is the closest energy to absolute acceptance of the prime creator—the God of the highest level of total trust in the process of creation. It has a power of Light that flows through all of the strands of the energy. Trust and generosity, these are the two key words that represent the Christ level. The Christ level is the highest expansion of the Light.

  "You can pray that your Christ level vision be activated. It is a combined energy of vision understanding and uncertainty. You have to accept the uncertainty that is the part of the Christ level vision to be activated. It has to do with faith.

The Christ level is absolute unity with the purpose and the concept of uncertainty, which permits change. When you pray for the Christ level to be activated, you need to permit yourself to watch your mind and open up for doubts to come in. You need to watch what your mind does and slowly quiet it down and open it up to absolute trust. Every soul has to ask for the activation of their Christ self. You can ask for everybody and see what happens."

Antichrist

- "Archangel Gabriel is saying that the antichrist is a concept in Christian religion. It does not exist in the same way in other religions. Every religion has the hierarchy of good and evil. In Christian religion, the evil has taken the form of antichrist. There can be many evil people representing the antichrist; it is the idea. Just like there are many Christs, similarly there can be many antichrists."

Natural and Manmade Disasters

Whenever I hear about a disaster of any kind anywhere on Earth, the first thing I do is pray to God and request the angels to help the spirits of the people who died to heaven, and to cleanse, heal, shield, and protect all those who got hurt and help their loved ones to cope with their loss, pain, and suffering. I also request the angels to cleanse, heal, and shield the places of disasters. When I heard about the massive mudslides in Guatemala and the earthquake in Pakistan and Northern India, and the other natural and manmade disasters, I prayed for the help for all the spirits and people involved. My patients described it as follows:

Mudslide in Guatemala

- "The whole area in Guatemala looks like a cake, and spirits are coming out of it. I also prayed for them, but it never occurred to me that they would be trapped there and could not come out of the mud, because they could not get out of the body. There are also spirits who are standing around the mud looking at it in shock. They were waiting for the other spirits to come out of the mud. With your prayers and the help of the angels, they are coming out and going to heaven. These spirits look as if they were pressed with a roller and appear flattened, elongated, and flimsy. It has to do with the type of trauma. On your request, the angels brought all their soul parts back and integrated them. Now they look normal and are being taken to heaven.

  "Angels lifted out all the foreign entities, dark shields, dark devices, and dark energies from everybody who was hurt, from all the family members and people who are affected by this tragedy and the whole area. Then they brought back everybody's soul parts back that were lost during this tragedy or other times, cleansed, healed, and filled them with the Light, and integrated them with those to whom they belonged. I see everybody involved as being healed.

"When you asked for the healing of the Earth, I saw a big heart and felt the pain of the Earth. It was as though a big piece had been pulled out from the chakra of the Earth. The angels brought all the soul parts to the Earth and its heart chakra and cleansed, healed, and filled them with the Light and integrated them where they belonged.

"I feel that healing is happening, and the heart pain is gone. The angels cleansed, healed, and shielded everybody and their surroundings with the triple net of Light, violet shield, metallic shield, mirror shields, and rays of blinding white Light. They opened everybody's connecting cords to God. My higher self is saying that bad things have happened here. In the past, human sacrifices were made here, and the place had some bad karma."

Earthquake in Pakistan

- "As you prayed, I saw that seconds before the earthquake in Pakistan occurred, many people had a flash of very bright Light and their souls came out of their bodies. If they had waited until after the earthquake, they would have been too panicky and their souls could not have come out of their bodies. That flash of Light calmed them down, and they calmly floated out of their bodies and began to rise up towards heaven. It was as if they had had a premonition with the flash of Light. I saw it happening to children in school. Almost all the souls of the children were on their way out of their bodies before the earthquake occurred, and they all went to heaven. Other spirits who did not leave are helped by the angels now at your request. I still see some people who are still alive and have not been found yet.

  "On your request the angels lifted out dark entities, dark devices, and dark energies from the earthquake areas, from the tectonic plates and from miles and miles around and helped them to the heaven. Then they filled the whole area and everybody and everything in it with the white Light. Angels also cleansed and healed everybody who was injured and all those who lost somebody, and brought all the soul parts back that they lost during the earthquake and after and integrated them with those to whom they belonged. They shielded them with the triple net of Light, violet shield, metallic shield, mirror shield, and rays of white Light. I see people who lost relatives also lost their soul parts, which are brought back by the angels and integrated with them after cleansing and healing. I feel the area is a lot calmer now. I feel the pressure has been released, but the tectonic plates are not realigned."

Volcanoes

When I prayed for healing of the volcanoes all over the earth and creation my hypnotized patients gave the following description:

- "When you prayed for volcanoes, I saw puffs of darkness coming out. The magnetic sheet was allowing for the lava to come out, but it was controlling how far the lava could come out, how high it would go, and then it would come down. Everything needs the flexibility to let off steam. There is darkness in layers, and you need to release them layer by layer. There is a time-release element in the darkness."

- "When Dr. Modi prayed to shield the volcano with multiple layers of triple compression chambers of crystalline Light, one on top of another all around the volcano and at the bottom, I saw it happening. They also put a filter on the top of the volcanoes, so it can filter out some gases, and some will stay on because it is part of the life expression of the volcanoes to have gas, lava, and fire. If they erupt, the shields will filter through the harmful gases, so it will not spread all over."

- "When Dr. Modi prayed for the volcano in the Pacific Ocean, which was erupting last week, by asking for several layers of protective shields to be put around it, so the gases would not spread all over, and also for a suction device on the top, so the harmful gases can be suctioned out and neutralized, I saw about 200 protective shields being put one over the other, at about twenty feet apart. These shields are about 4,000 feet high. I see gases going straight up and not from the sides. The spaces between the shields have something like pores, and the gases are dissipating and are not toxic anymore. The shields are acting as filters. They filter out negative gases as they pass through each shield and are not harmful anymore. I also saw the volcano under the water; it was going slowly horizontally and was dissipating in the water without causing a force to create the tsunami."

• "Now I am focusing on the volcano in the Philippines that I saw in the news yesterday. It is just erupting a little bit; it is not a big one. When you prayed for the cleansing and healing of the tectonic plates and the volcano with the magnetic sheets, I kept on sensing the tremendous anger in the volcano and the tectonic plates that was caused by the dark entities and energies. They were all ejected, transformed, and taken to heaven and all their missing soul parts were brought back with the magnetic sheets around them. I see all the anger is dissipated, and the volcano is calmer. This time, the angels are putting different types of shields around the volcano.

"Archangel Gabriel is saying that if we can imagine a spinning top, the energy around the top is horizontal while the top is vertical. Shields have a top and the bottom. If you were to leave the volcano as it is without the shield, the lava and gases will come out vertically at the point where it stops. It goes through layers to the atmosphere. When the shield is put on, it does not go down with that force because downward movement is broken by all these horizontal filters that are built in the horizontal shields. We were calling them filters, but they are inside of the original horizontal shields. The inside of the shield is composed of different curves like garden hoses, like big spaghetti with holes in them through which gases go at different levels. The force and the concentration of these gases make them harmful, but when they just go through filters in the shields, they dissipate. It is like a transmutation of the harsh angry energy."

- "When Dr. Modi spoke to all the volcanoes all over the earth and creation that all their anger is because of the demonic influence, which has just been taken out and to be in peace and relax and that they have a purpose to maintain the balance. I saw volcanoes relaxing and realizing that they do not have to make noise. They could take their own responsibility for their balance within the Earth. Volcanoes need to erupt from time to time, but if we cleanse, heal, and shield them, then the eruption will be mild."

Tornadoes

- "Sometimes explosive results are needed to release the pressure. If we cleanse, heal, and shield the air, atmosphere, ocean, and everything connected with it, they can be weakened. I see that tornadoes and disasters sometimes are necessary to wake people up. I see the air before cleansing and healing was turbulent, and there were grayish forms, and after cleansing, the forms are not gray any more. They are much lighter."

Tectonic Plates

During a session as I prayed for the healing of the tectonic plates, my patient described it as follows:

- "Earthquakes are like shaking and shivering of the Earth. Beside the tectonic plates moving, there are demons in the tectonic plates that are creating a lot of angry feelings in them, which leads to the earthquakes. When the magnetic sheets are put around them, they ejected the darkness from the tectonic plates, which are collected in the net of Light, transformed, and taken to heaven. I see demons with horns and tails coming out of them. They have long, sharp claws in the toes, and on the heel, they have spurs. Billions of them are coming out of the tectonic plates in Earth. Then all the soul parts are attracted back from everywhere in the creation: from Satan, his demons, from people, places, darkness, and heaven from this time and space and beyond. I see many soul parts coming back to the tectonic plates in the Earth. Like the humans, it is not going to change immediately.

"When the darkness which holds in the feelings of anger is lifted from the tectonic plates, then there is relaxation and calmness in them. Anger is energy, it is power, is a force that it holds things together in a very strong, dark way which can break off easily. There is more flexibility when there is no anger. Therefore, the way the tectonic plates would work is that they become softer. They don't need to send out that kind of energy of their movement, their brutality, and power to the water, and everything that is surrounding them. It can relax and stay still. Then when you shielded them with triple compression chamber of crystalline Light, violet shield, mirror shields, and rays of blinding white Light, it protects, softens, and quiets them down. I hear the triple compression chamber of crystalline Light saying to the tectonic plates to calm down. They have instructions programmed in them. It rumbles a little because it has the memory. Also, we can pray for everything that is affected by the movements of the tectonic plates. All this healing will slow the movements and thus there will be fewer and less powerful earthquakes.

"Archangel Gabriel is saying that we humans need to ask for healing again and again, more than once. Even though when you ask once it starts to happen, you have to ask frequently to get enough of an understanding and enough answers. When enough of the people get it, including the Earth around the tectonic plates, the air, the water, and the gas, then when you start to look at it, it begins to happen. You can also ask everything around that is affected by the movements of tectonic plates to be cleansed, healed, and shielded. All these will slow the earthquakes.

"Once you understand what tectonic plates are there for and you take out the darkness, fill them with the Light and shield them, so that they can evolve into the Light, it still will have some negativity in it but will not be so dark and angry. It will have a different quality. It will slow down and will not react with so much anger and violence."

- "When you, Dr. Modi, prayed for tectonic plates, I see separate magnetic sheets around each plate to keep it from moving too fast and too quick. They are given some leg room to move; they have to move; they will change as time evolves. This time, not much darkness came out like before and they looked calmer and more peaceful. I only see little black pebble type of energy in them. I get that they will be released in time."

Earthquake Near Indonesia

- "When Dr. Modi prayed for the magnetic sheets to be put around the earthquake area near Indonesia on April 11, 2012, tectonic plates, volcanoes, water creatures and plant life and the land all around the ocean, I saw angels putting extra magnetic sheets that looked like saran wrap around those areas affected by the earthquake. They were using some kind of torch, like you would use for soldering metals to close up some holes in the magnetic sheets. Then when she asked, the switch to the magnetic sheets to be turned on to the 'eject' sign, I saw like the other times a black liquid type of energy and black blobs coming out from everywhere including the earthquake areas.

  "As I look at the tectonic plates I see multitudes of dark blobs and black liquid coming out of them and the surrounding areas and everything and everybody in that area. They were collected in the net of Light and taken to heaven. Then when she asked the switch to the tectonic plates to turn to the 'attract' sign, I saw soul parts returning to the tectonic plates, ocean and all the life forms in it and the land around and everything and everybody in them including all those who died, got hurt or lost loved ones, from Satan, his demons, all their dark storage and working places, and from people, places and heaven. They were cleansed, healed, filled with the Light and integrated with whom they belonged and where they belonged. I see that there was a massive fragmentation occurring to everybody and everything in the area and it has been healed. Angels are saying that we need to ask for cleansing and healing more than just one time to remove the darkness from all the layers and bring everything and everybody's soul parts, to heal the area and beings in it.

"I saw God infusing love, Light, hope and peace into everything and everybody affected by the earthquake on Dr. Modi's request. I also saw God infusing a lot of kindness as well through everybody's connecting cord to make people kind to one another during the tragedy due to the earthquake.

"When Dr. Modi prayed to stabilize the tectonic plates, I saw angel putting a flexible zipper in the tectonic plates so the tectonic plates can still move but they are held gently together. I saw it happening to the tectonic plates all over the Earth.

"I saw people panicking and screaming all over during the earthquake. I also saw the tsunami started right away but was weak and far away from the land around. When Dr. Modi prayed to God to do whatever needs to be done to stop this tsunami or make it weak, I saw heaven absorbing massive amounts of energy that was coming out from under the ocean and the Earth. I saw angels putting a sheet of metal that sucked and absorbed the energy and calmed the tsunami waves. What I get is that now it will not reach the land.

"I saw violet liquid fire flowing throughout the areas of the earthquake and all over the earth and creation healing and transforming everything and everybody. Then angels shielded the whole creation and everything and everybody in it including the earthquake area with the triple compression chamber of crystalline Light, mirror shield and the violet shield."

Radioactive Contamination

When I prayed for healing of nuclear power plants, patient described it as follows:

- "When Dr. Modi prayed to put the magnetic sheets around all the nuclear power plants throughout the Earth including the one in Japan, and suction out all the radioactive material which might be leaking, I saw it happening all over the Earth. I saw a very bright hose of white Light coming down from heaven and then it divided into many mini hoses all over the Earth, pulling stuff from every direction and all going into one big hose up to the heaven and transforming into the Light.

"I saw all the radioactive material from the atmosphere, water and everywhere else being sucked out, transformed and taken to heaven. Also the dark energy was coming out of all the emotions and thoughts such as: responses to the negative events and heart break from the deaths and destruction. The dark energy was also coming out of all the negative practices such as, voodoo, witchcraft, spells, animal and human sacrifices. I saw dark energy coming out of all types of trash, even the medical trash such as: needles, gloves, body parts etc. Also the energy of death, murder, rape and the emotions connected with that being sucked out. It was like a hurricane of emotions being sucked out. A lot of negative energy was collected on Earth and took a long time to suction them out."

Other Ideas for Prayers and Healing

Healing of Earth

- "Archangel Gabriel is saying to pray to help you to dig deeper into structures of the Earth for more details, which will go all over the creation, based on the formula or the energy level. When we say formula, we mean energy level. When you heal the Earth, you will discover the formulas—the energy levels which will then be applicable. The energy is consistent. The order and how much energy is sent varies.

  "There are layers and layers and levels of application of Light, which are interfered with and have demonic presence. Your job is to send the demons to the Light. The layers are created by the combinations of energy. Once you discover a layer, you will discover the formula for the energy of that layer. That combination of the energy has a different application wherever it is on other planets because it is Light. We are talking about the qualities of Light. For example, each strand of DNA has a different quality of Light with the different instructions, so each layer is also a particular combination of Light. The opposition energy is the dark energy or the interference. Once that is lifted, it will be lifted from that same formula wherever it applies. You need to find where you want to go next. Just keep going until you are satisfied."

Healing of Reptilians

- "When Dr. Modi prayed for the Earth, I also saw reptilian beings that were quite large in size living in the deeper layers of the Earth. They look like alligators, but they are on their two hind legs; they are not crawling on their stomachs. I see the angels putting the magnetic sheets tightly around these reptilian beings. I can see a lot of dark beings and dark energy being ejected out of them, and a lot of soul parts are brought back to them from everywhere."

Terrorists

- "When you prayed for terrorists' healing, it is happening a little bit at a time, because they have closed down. You can talk to their higher selves about the common idea that binds them together and what they believe their power to be. The demonic energy in them is very powerful. Work with the demon commander of terrorists of the Earth. There are all different types of terrorists, such as the rednecks, Nazis, policemen, criminals, psychopaths and many more, who have closed down completely any feelings of compassion. There are demon subcommanders for each of these categories. Some of them you have already worked with, but there are more you need to work with. When you prayed for terrorists of every kind in every part of society, beginning with the family, I saw darkness coming out of them like a volcano."

Gifts

- "When you asked for different types of gifts, I saw a golden orange Light come down inside, and then it would come up like a drawing of a tree with branches and leaves which are curved. Each branch of the tree is a different form of knowledge and gift, then it becomes like files of all the possibilities in each of them. It is almost like a Christmas tree with gifts hanging on it. They are activated when you asked for them.

    "When you asked in prayers for abundance for everybody, the angels and the Light came and did the work. It is like when you are asking for abundance for countries and people in poverty, the angels go there and do the work with a greater capacity. By the act of your asking, they can assist you in the process.

"When you asked for the divine sense of humor, I saw it being poured. There are certain angels of humor who spread divine joy, humor, and laughter, imparting these qualities in people. They come around and spread joy and happiness in and around people, transmit certain qualities and thoughts, and inspire divine joy and humor in them.

"When you asked for different gifts, I saw a horn of abundance and different gifts with different colors pouring out to us and to all the other people throughout creation. I saw rivers of pink, blue, green, and other colors pouring from the horn of plenty [these will be explained in detail in a future publication]. When you asked for the gift of deep inner peace and faith in God, which nothing and nobody can shake, I saw a Light of blue color going in you, and anchoring and strengthening your faith in God. Sometimes it can be reinforced through your solar plexus so that your emotions are not shaken when you have this alignment with God.

"As you asked for humility and other gifts, they poured out of the horn of plenty. I saw two angels come down and put a royal blue velvety cape on your shoulders. It had gold trimming and braiding around the edges. It is to assist you in your work with writing and communicating. It has divine qualities, which you can impart when needed. It also has a protective function to protect you and your work because of your divine purpose.

"The angels also put a sort of crown over your head because you do a lot of work in helping God and heaven, and it is appreciated. It is also a protection for you. It is a divine tool that is embedded with qualities of God and the Light. You were given a wand, like the fairy godmother, and I saw you using it. As you were asking for all these gifts, it opened many avenues in your life. I saw that on the spiritual level your head was bowed with humility. It is an act of asking. You have the special gifts of intuition and knowing what to ask for. By keeping the head bowed with humility, you are like a facilitator for the process."

Mind

- "Archangel Gabriel is saying the brain feeds the mind, so it can operate in the physical body. The mind is outside of the body but also in the body, so there is a need for the connection between the two. The connection between the two is the knowing, the spirit that feeds the mind and the brain that feeds the body. The mind is in heaven where the Akashic records are. When it works with the brain, it forgets it is operating on the human level, but it also has access to all the information of the universe, everything that is ever known. It is not totally in this dimension, it is an interphase. It is in both.

  "It is like that veil/net, gold on one side and gray on the other. The gray has been layered and that is the part that is in the Earth. When it is in the world without so much of the demonic energy, it is like the white veil. This is how the mind operates in the three-dimensional worlds. It is like a transformer when you have electricity in one country and the other and it does not match, you have to have the transformer to match it. That is what the tube is between the mind and the brain. Sometimes the tube can be made larger or smaller, but as long as there is flow, and if there is a door, it is easy to open. For you it is better to have a constant flow instead of the door because you are in connection to divinity, to heaven. If you have it feeding you, then you can know more, like a connection with the Akashic records. Seeing the mind in the forehead is the third-dimensional adjustment where the separation of individual talents and expression will be satisfactory to God. God wants you to expand, enjoy life, play and have fun, and learn new things."

Joy

- "When Dr. Modi prayed for boundless joy for everybody in creation, I saw a fountain of pinkish shimmering Light erupting from the center of the Earth and spreading all over the Earth. I am also seeing a fountain of pinkish Light erupting from the soul of every human being, filling them with joy. Fountains of Light are also erupting through each and every dimension and in everybody in them, spreading the love and joy all over. When you prayed for joy to be flooded throughout the creation, I saw beautiful little flowers all coming down and spreading joy."

Past Life Personalities

- "As Dr. Modi asked all my past-life personalities to be brought back and integrated with me after cleansing and healing, I see them coming from nowhere, as if they are coming from another dimension to this dimension. My higher self is saying that these past-life personalities are coming from a lot of different places. Past life personality is in spirit form, it is not a part of your soul, but it is made up of the same soul essence. It is your personality of a life. It has knowledge of that past life. It is like the outer shell of a past life. It can be in heaven, on Earth, in the universe, in an aura, or near the body somewhere. When we resolve the issues from those past lives and bring back and integrate all the missing soul parts, we then can integrate the past-life personality along with its knowledge and gifts. The more past lives we resolve and heal, the more past-life personalities are integrated, the more knowledge and gifts we have, and the more whole we become."

Guidelines for the Protection Prayers

Over the years, I realized that during a hypnotherapy session, the patient and my higher self, heavenly guides, angels, masters, and other heavenly beings are always present, even if we are not aware of them. They are assigned to educate, guide, and protect us if we ask. Because of the demonic interferences during the session, I always begin the sessions with a protection prayer. I often use the following guidelines for prayers.

- Invoke power and presence of God, patient, and my angels, higher self, heavenly guides, masters, and oversoul with whom we are connected, Also higher self, angels, guides, and masters of every soul and dimension throughout the creation.

- Request the angels to put the magnetic sheets around the whole creation and heaven and everything and everybody in them, including me and my family members.

- Around every universe, galaxy, solar system, parallel universe, sun, moon, star, asteroid, comet, planet, black hole, inter- and intra-dimensional pathway, dimension that used to be hell and is now the dimension of Light, space that used to be purgatory and other spaces used by Satan and his demons.

- Around Satan, his demons, his warehouses and working places, all the dark portals all over the earth and the creation and in every person, and all the dark places they lead to.

- Around every planet including the Earth and all the parallel dimensions around the Earth, around every country, state, district, city, town, and village, and around every structure and monument.

- Around every home and building and every room, hallway, attic, basement and everything and everybody in them, including all the electrical and electronic appliances and gadgets, electrical powerhouses, outlets, and all the satellite stations.

- Put magnetic sheets around volcanoes, tectonic plates, water bodies such as rivers, ponds, waterfalls and oceans; all the forests, mountains and desert areas; all the streets, farmlands, drinking water sources and land all over, air and atmosphere and all the natural and created vortexes all over and around the Earth and creation and under every home, building, street, land, and water body.

- Around all cars and transportation vehicles and their stations and parking lots.

- Activate all the magnetic sheets all around the creation and heaven and everything and everybody in them.

- Turn the switch of the magnetic sheets to the Eject sign.

- Pray to eject everything from our mind, body, and soul that is responsible for all our physical, emotional, mental, spiritual, and relationship problems.

- Eject all the foreign spirits, dark shields, dark devices, dark connections, dark blocks, and dark energy, all the infectious organisms of every type. Eject everything from every system, every organ, every part, skin, muscles, bones, joints, nails, teeth, gums, tongue, throat, voice box, scalp, hair follicles and hair, endocrine glands, and all the aging hormones, gray hair pigments, aging cells, and aging tissues.

- Eject everything that is responsible for our ego, arrogance, feelings of superiority, inferiority, shame, guilt, selfish and self-centered thoughts and behavior, desire to control others, desire to judge or criticize others and ourselves, desire to hurt others and ourselves, anxiety, fears and phobias of every type, anger, hate, jealousy, paranoia, psychosis, depression, Tourette's syndrome, autism, manic depression, obsessive-compulsive thoughts and behavior, addictions to drugs, alcohol, food, tobacco, cigarettes,

155

sex, gambling, and money. Eject all the darkness from all our memories, thoughts, and behaviors.

- Eject everything responsible for our unresolved physical, emotional, mental, spiritual, and relationship problems, coming from our past lives.

- Eject everything that should not be there from all our kundalini, meridians, nadis, chakras, psychic antennas, grids, all 32 strands of our DNA, all the connecting cords between all the souls and dimensions in the creation and heaven, from all our physical, mental, emotional, and spiritual bodies.

- Eject everything that should not be there from all the areas of natural and manmade disasters and everybody who is affected by the disasters and the surroundings.

- Collect everything ejected in the net of Light, transform them, and take them to heaven.

- Pray to God to flood the whole creation and heaven and everything and everybody in them and all around them with the white, crystalline, liquid Light and let it remove everything that is left over.

- Turn the switch of the magnetic sheet to the Attract sign.

- Allow all the missing soul parts to come back from Satan, his demons, people, places, darkness, and heaven, from this time and space and beyond, which we lost in this life and all the other lifetimes from the beginning of our existence and creation of our soul.

- Cleanse them, heal them, fill them with the Light, and integrate them with whom or where they belong.

- Clamp the cord to the missing soul parts, which cannot be brought back at this time, twenty or more times.

- Pray to God to flood the whole creation and heaven and everything and everybody in them with the violet, liquid fire and let it blaze into intense violet flame and heal and realign all our DNA.

156

- Create Light centers everywhere we have put the magnetic sheets all over the creation.

- Shield the whole creation and heaven and everything and every-body in them, including where the dark portals were, with the triple compression chambers of crystalline, white Light.

- Let the youth hormones flow through the whole body and reverse the aging process of every soul, including me and my family members, friends, and each and every human being.

- Pray to God to activate our mind, body and soul, all the con-necting cords to God, masters, guardian angels, heavenly guides, higher self, inner self, Akashic records, and to every soul in the creation and heaven. Also activate the grid system, kundalini, meridians, nadis, twelve major and all the minor chakras, psychic antennas, all the brain centers and thirty-two strands of DNA, and every cell and infuse them with the crys-talline, golden, liquid Light.

- Activate and open all the psychic abilities as needed and shield and protect them when not needed.

- Activate my Christ self and Christ self-vision. Do this for every soul throughout the creation.

- Expand the Light in Satan and his demons.

Protection Prayer

Sit in a comfortable position and take three slow, deep breaths. Then you can either read this protection prayer aloud or record it on a cassette tape and listen to it every night before sleeping and in the morning after you wake up.

I pray to God and request the angels to please put the magnetic sheets around the whole creation and heaven, and everything and everybody in them, including my family members and myself. Put them around the void all around the creation and heaven and in between them, around the space that was used by Satan as purgatory and the space under that; around the dimension that used to be hell, but now is a dimension of Light; all around the universes, galaxies, solar systems, parallel universes, planets, suns, moons, stars, comets, asteroids, intra- and inter-dimensional pathways, black holes, the whole Earth, and all the parallel dimensions or worlds around it; around all the continents, countries, states, districts, cities, towns, and villages; all the homes, buildings, structures, streets, and everything in between.

Put the magnetic sheets around all the buildings, such as schools and other educational buildings of every kind; prison buildings, courtrooms and legal buildings; healing places such as hospitals, mental institutions, nursing homes, medical clinics and doctors' offices; all of the worship places; bars, and places of recreation, gambling places, brothels; graveyards, funeral homes, and crematoriums; all the transportation vehicles and their stations and parking places; government buildings, science, and research buildings; all the electrical power sources, electrical and electronic appliances and gadgets, including the computers, printers and televisions; satellite stations, nuclear power plants; all the political and religious leaders and their homes, offices, and cars; museums, art centers, buildings related to motion pictures, all of the buildings, places and areas of entertainment; all libraries, publishing companies and bookstores; all the news media buildings, such as television stations, radio stations and buildings for newspapers and magazines; and all the other buildings and around every room, attic, basement, and hallway in every building and home.

Put the magnetic sheets around all the volcanoes, tectonic plates, water bodies such as rivers, ponds, waterfalls, and oceans; all the forests, mountains and desert areas; all the streets, farmlands, drinking water sources, and land all over; air and atmosphere; all the natural and created vortexes all over and around the earth and creation and under every home, building, street, and land.

Also, put the magnetic sheets around all the areas of natural and manmade disasters; areas of conflict, war zones, all the living and training areas of people in the navy, army, and air force; around all the ships, planes, cars, trains, buses, spaceships on the ground and in space, and all other transportation vehicles and their stations and parking places; around the mind, body, and soul of all the humans, aliens, elementals, animals, insects, reptilians, plant life, and creatures of every kind; around every system, every part, every organ, every endocrine gland, and thirty-two strands of our DNA; around our kundalini, meridians, nadis, chakras, psychic antennas, grid system all over the creation; the physical, emotional, mental, and spiritual bodies; and all the connecting cords between every soul and dimension throughout the creation and heaven.

Put the magnetic sheet around Satan, his demons, their warehouses, and the dark portals in every place and every person and the dark places they lead to. I request the angels to please activate all the magnetic sheets that are put around the whole creation and heaven, and everything and everybody in them, including around me, my family members, all our homes, workplaces, and cars. Turn the switch on the magnetic sheets to the Eject sign and expel all the foreign entities, dark shields, dark devices, dark energies, and infectious agents of every type, everything is responsible for our weight problems and allergies to different foods, etc.

Eject everything negative from every system, every part, every organ, every endocrine gland, from all the thirty-two strands of DNA, kundalini, meridians, nadis, twelve major and all the minor chakras, psychic antenna and all the connecting cord to God and Light, masters, angels, heavenly guides, higher self, inner-self, Akashic records, to the Earth, and to every soul and dimension throughout the creation and heaven.

Also eject everything that is responsible for our ego, arrogance, feelings of superiority, inferiority, prejudice, anger, hate, jealousy, guilt, shame, selfish and self-centered thoughts and behavior, feelings of rejection, addictions to drugs, alcohol, sex, food, gambling, money and other things; fears, phobias, anxiety, panic attacks, depression, perfectionism, obsessive-compulsive thoughts and behavior, paranoia, psychosis, desire to judge and criticize others and ourselves, desire for revenge and desire to hurt others and ourselves, desire to scream at and control other people, Tourette's syndrome, autism; lack of confidence, shyness, and all mental, physical, emotional, spiritual, and relationship problems.

Eject everything responsible for our unresolved physical, emotional, mental, spiritual, and relationship problems coming from this life and all our past lives from the beginning of our existence, and all our negative thoughts, decisions, and promises made during all the past lives.

"Eject all the aging hormones, aging tissues and cells, gray hair pigment, and let the youth hormones flow through our body and reverse the aging process.

I request the angels to collect everything that is ejected in the net of Light, transform them, and take them to heaven, please.

I pray to God to please flood the whole creation and heaven, and everything and everybody in them, the void all around the creation and heaven and in between the dimensions with the white, crystalline, liquid Light; cleansing, healing, and removing everything that is left over, from the whole creation and heaven and everything and everybody in them, including me and my family members.

Then I request the angels to turn the switch of all the magnetic sheets to the Attract sign and allow all the missing soul parts that we lost in this life and all the other lifetimes, from the beginning of our existence, to come back from Satan, his demons, people, places, darkness, from heaven, from this time and space and beyond. Allow them to integrate with whom or wherever they belong after thoroughly cleansing and healing them.

Clamp all the cords to the missing soul parts that cannot be brought back at this time, twenty or more times. Turn the switch to the neutral position.

I pray to God to please fill the whole creation and everything and everybody in the creation, and all around the creation, with the violet liquid fire and let it blaze into intense flames and heal and realign our DNA.

Shield everything and everybody throughout the creation, including myself, my family members, friends, coworkers, and all our homes, workplaces, cars, and the places where the dark portals were in people and places.

Create the Light centers all around the creation and everything where the magnetic sheets are placed.

Please infuse all the connecting cords between every soul and dimension throughout the creation and heaven with the crystalline, golden, liquid Light, and remove everything that does not belong there.

Please cleanse, heal, and shield all the chakras, kundalini, meridians, nadis, psychic antennas and our physical, emotional, mental, and spiritual bodies, with triple compression chambers of crystalline Light. Open them when needed and close and shield them when not needed, please.

I pray to God to please cleanse, heal, and bless the food, drink, medicine, and everything I consume and the air I breathe, so they can be beneficial for my mind, body, and soul.

Please increase everybody's immune system to the maximum level.

I pray to God to please activate my Christ self and Christ self-vision. Do this for every soul and dimension throughout the creation.

Shakuntala Modi, M.D.

Please cleanse, heal, and activate all our kundalini, chakras, meridians, etheric nadis and their pressure points, psychic antennas, physical, emotional, mental, and spiritual bodies, all thirty-two strands of DNA, including the self-healing strand of DNA, and all the channels of communication with God, masters, higher self, inner self, heavenly guides, angels, and other heavenly beings, with the Akashic records; all our heart, blood and all the blood vessels, lymphatic vessels, brain and every center of the brain, every part and organ of the body, mind and soul of every human, alien and all the other souls, and also connections to all the souls and the earth and other dimensions, and infuse them with the crystalline, golden, liquid Light.

Make all the biological, chemical, and nuclear weapons ineffective and bring peace and harmony all over the Earth and the whole creation.

I pray to God to please bless me, all my family members, friends, all the people around them, all the humans, and everything and everybody in the whole creation, with an abundance of whatever we need, including food, shelter, daily necessities, money, job, unconditional love and forgiveness towards ourselves and everybody around us, deep inner peace and faith in God that nobody and nothing can shake, boundless joy, happiness, energy, motivation, kindness, compassion, and humility. Please bless us with all the gifts we need to fulfill our purpose, including gifts of intuition, inspiration, patience, good sense of humor and good physical, emotional, mental, and spiritual health.

I request the angels stay on guard around me and my family members, friends, coworkers, and each and every human being, living being, and our homes, workplaces and cars, and all the other transportation vehicles, in this dimension and in all the other dimensions, to protect us and guide us in the right direction as long as our soul exist, please.

You have my permission to take any action on my behalf to protect me and my family members and every human and living being as long as our soul exists.

162

I form an intent not to be possessed and influenced by any spirit and reject all the works of Satan and his demons and human and alien beings under their influences.

I also form an intent to accept the works of God and achieve God's purposes and to achieve my goals and purposes that I planned in the Light by dedicating my life to God.

I pray to God to please fill the whole creation and everybody and everything in the creation, including the whole Earth and everything and everybody in it, including myself and all my family members and friends and all the human beings, other living beings, and their homes, workplaces, cars, and everything and everybody in them with the violet liquid fire, like violet lava. Please let it transmute and heal all the karmic problems with my family members, friends, coworkers, and all the other people in my life, so we can live in peace and harmony.

Do this for every soul throughout the creation for the good of everybody.

And now, imagine a column of brilliant, dazzling, shimmering, vibrant, relaxing, and healing, white, crystalline Light coming from above your head from God. Watch it going through your head, permeating and healing each and every part and organ of your body, from the top of your head to the tips of your fingers and toes, pushing out and removing all the human, demon, alien, and other foreign entities, dark shields, dark devices, dark energies, dark connections, all the negative thoughts and desires, and all your anxiety, fears and worries out of your mind, body, aura, cord, soul, and surroundings. Just imagine your whole body lighting up like a powerful Light bulb.

Now imagine this Light spreading an arm's length all around you, below your feet, above your head, in front of you, behind you and on both sides of you—creating a brilliant, dazzling, shimmering bubble of crystalline Light or tube of Light all around you and your silver cord to God.

Imagine this shield covered with a triple compression chamber of crystalline Light, spiritual mirrors, and rays of brilliant, vibrant, white, crystalline Light.

You and only you have a right to live in this body and shield. If anybody or anything tries to enter your shield, you will be aware of it at the subconscious level of your mind. Instead of allowing them into your shield, you will request the angels to remove and send them where they belong.

Now imagine the violet, liquid fire pouring like a violet lava from God through your connecting silver cord in and around you like a waterfall, permeating and penetrating your mind, soul, and every part, every organ, every cell and DNA of your body and soul, igniting into intense violet flames, spreading in you and all around you, all through your home, workplaces, cars, and everything and everybody in them, and miles and miles around them, nonstop, twenty-four hours a day.

Also, visualize the violet flame blazing through your family members, friends, coworkers, people who harmed you, people whom you harmed, and even your enemies.

Put all your day-to-day problems and issues, including all your physical, emotional, mental, spiritual, and relationship problems, in the violet fire, and they can be resolved and transformed.

Imagine yourself, your family members, friends, coworkers and all humans and their homes, workplaces, and cars shining like a brilliant, dazzling afternoon sun.

Afterthoughts

Doing this work for about twenty-five years, I have learned that all communication between God and us passes through our silver connecting cords. When we pray, our prayers ascend through our cords to God. God hears and answers our prayers through this "cosmic umbilical cord." Information is always flowing through this cord, whether we are aware of it or not. I am thoroughly convinced that it is very important to pray for protection and guidance daily. While individual prayers are important, group prayers have incredible impact. It is very important for family members to pray, both individually and together, for protection, healing, and guidance for themselves and for all the people in their lives. Praying for other people sometimes is more powerful, because it is selfless.

As controversial as the subject is, prayers are especially important in schools. Prayers do not have to be based on any religion; they can be to a higher power of the Light. When we pray, a column of Light and love floods from God to us and our surroundings through our silver connecting cords. The demon spirits are afraid of the Light and cannot come close to it. If we keep our children and schools filled and illuminated with God's Light through prayers, they can be protected from negative demonic influences. It is important to remember that where there is no Light, darkness will rule. This is what is happening in our schools without prayers.

According to the heavenly beings, no prayers in school is one of the most important reasons why our children are becoming rebellious and violent, and why they are indulging in drugs, alcohol, and self-destructive and antisocial behaviors. Through prayers in schools, we can fill them with the Light, and our kids can remain clear of all the dark influences that plague them. It is particularly important to teach our children these protection prayers, not out of fear but out of awareness.

We must keep our children clear of demonic influences through prayers and thereby keep them away from drugs, alcohol, violence, and other self-destructive and antisocial behaviors. This way, we can build a loving and peaceful society. Prayers are our open line to God. God will protect and guide us and will listen to and answer our prayers, but we must ask. Instead of creating conflicts about which prayer to use and which religious figure to pray to, pray to one Almighty God or Supreme Being most religions believe in, rather than not praying at all and allowing Satan and his demons to rule us, our schools, and our society.

According to heavenly beings, when we pray for healing, it is often given, but the problem is that it gets rejected. We have to work on accepting it by changing our ways. All prayers are heard, no matter how superficial they are. Sometimes they are not answered right away or the way we want, because there is a lesson to be learned from what is going on in our lives. The answer to a prayer depends on our life plan. God granted us free will to learn the lessons and grow spiritually. God does not interfere with our free will. Asking for God's help is an exercise of our free will. God is all-knowing, but He will not intervene unless we ask.

Besides praying for ourselves and our loved ones, we also need to pray for every soul throughout the creation and heaven, because we are all connected with each other by connecting cords. People under hypnosis describe it as a spider web connecting every soul with each other and with God. We are all pieces of God. If we can imagine God as one body, then we are like different cells and parts of that body of God. When any part of that body hurts, the whole body hurts. Similarly, when we hurt any other person, we hurt ourselves as well. We must treat each other with love and care in order to preserve the whole. Love is the most powerful source in the universe. When we give love, we also receive it, and as it moves back and forth, it grows and provides the healing for everybody involved. Only love can heal, and it is the only thing which really matters.

With prayers, we can also transform the demons into the Light and send them to heaven; thus, we will have fewer problems to deal with. As explained in my first book, *Remarkable Healings*, demons are also part of the same body of God. They are the lost souls and need our prayers and help for their transformation.

According to the heavenly beings, what happens in the future is in our hands. We have to know that with the help of God through prayers, we have the power to prevent massive destruction. The choice is ours, and God and the heavenly beings cannot interfere with our free will. We should all pray and meditate regularly and include God in our daily life, not just when there is a tragedy.

CPSIA information can be obtained at www.ICGtesting.com
Printed in the USA
BVOW11s1438281215

431152BV00002B/85/P

9 781618 979476